Good Housekeeping

MIDWEEK
LIFESAVERS

WHEN USING KITCHEN APPLIANCES PLEASE ALWAYS
FOLLOW THE MANUFACTURER'S INSTRUCTIONS

HarperCollins*Publishers*
1 London Bridge Street
London SE1 9GF

www.harpercollins.co.uk

HarperCollins*Publishers*
Macken House, 39/40 Mayor Street Upper
Dublin 1, D01 C9W8, Ireland

First published by HarperCollins*Publishers* 2024

1 3 5 7 9 10 8 6 4 2

Text and photography © Good Housekeeping 2024

Project director: Gaby Huddart
Project editor: Tracy Müller-King

Recipe writers: Meike Beck, Emma Franklin, Alice Shields,
Grace Evans, Georgie D'Arcy Coles, Lucy Jessop, Suzannah Butcher,
Elizabeth Fox, Sophie Austen-Smith, Monaz Dumasia, Charlotte Watson,
Madeline Burkitt, Gabriella English, Zoe Garner, Olivia Spurrell

Photographers: Alex Luck, Mike English, Kris Kirkham, Will Heap,
Nassima Rothacker, Myles New, Kate Whitaker, Philip Webb, Debi Treloar,
Steve Baxter, Gareth Morgans, Tom Regester, Oscar Hather
Vinny Whiteman, Brett Stevens

Good Housekeeping asserts the moral right to be identified as the
author of this work

A catalogue record of this book is available from the British Library

ISBN 978-0-00-870201-4

Printed and bound by GPS Group

This book contains FSC™ certified paper and other controlled
sources to ensure responsible forest management.

For more information visit: www.harpercollins.co.uk/green

Good Housekeeping
MIDWEEK
LIFESAVERS

130 EASY, SPEEDY RECIPES TO REVITALISE
YOUR WEEKNIGHT DINNERS

HarperCollins*Publishers*

Contents

Foreword by Gaby Huddart, Editor-at-large

When the Good Housekeeping team and I were discussing the subject of this year's cookery book, we bounced around all sorts of ideas in answer to current trends. A vegan tome, an air-fryer special, a bible of chocolate recipes... or perhaps a celebration of the most popular dishes of the past 100 years to mark the 100th anniversary of the Good Housekeeping Institute?

But day in, day out, what our readers come to us for more than anything else is midweek dinner inspiration. Whether in our magazine, on our website, via one of our e-newsletters or app, the most in-demand recipes are always those for easy, fast and delicious midweek meals. There's a visible spike in visits when a new suggestion goes up online, and I've often received emails to thank me for simple new flavoursome recipes in *Good Housekeeping* magazine – many with proud photos of readers' own renditions of the dishes.

But why is this demand so marked? I think it's a sign of two things. Firstly, there's the busyness epidemic that afflicts so many of us these days. Juggling work, home, family, friends, finances and life generally has got a lot of people maxed out. Diaries are crammed full to bursting and, when it comes to dinnertime, people want to serve up something tasty that doesn't require hours of slaving over a stove. Most of us have a handful of dishes we know how to make by heart, but nobody wants to eat the same meals again and again on repeat – we all want to keep our tastebuds entertained! And when our days are packed with making decisions on a myriad of things, it's a blessed relief to have somewhere to turn to when it comes to choosing what to prepare for dinner.

Secondly, over the past year or two there has been a rapidly growing awareness of just how important it is for our health to eat freshly prepared meals, rather than turning to convenience and processed foods. Indeed, it's been impossible to avoid recent headlines about the dangers of ultra-processed foods (UPFs), and there's a growing body of evidence suggesting that they could be as dangerous to our wellbeing as smoking or drinking alcohol to excess. In a study by the *British Medical Journal*, no fewer than 32 different health risks were identified from regular consumption of UPFs – which include things like ice cream, sausages, crisps, mass-produced bread, breakfast cereals, instant soups, biscuits and fruit-flavoured yogurts. And yet, UPFs are estimated to make up 57% of the UK diet – perhaps not surprising when one considers that they are often cheap and palate-pleasing. Clearly, anyone making meals for people they love can't help but take on board the importance of cooking from scratch – at least most of the time (we do recognise that we all need to cheat sometimes).

And that's why we felt this book really was a no-brainer! We've carefully selected more than 130 brilliant recipes that you can turn to as 'midweek lifesavers' – mouth-watering in terms of flavour, but straightforward in terms of the skill and effort required to make them. Just as importantly, most of them are ready in well under an hour, ensuring time in the kitchen is kept to a minimum.

Being a Good Housekeeping cookbook, all the recipes also come with our Triple Tested promise. What does this mean? Quite simply that every recipe is guaranteed to work every time. Our amazing cookery director, Meike Beck, and her team of professionally trained cookery developers and writers leave absolutely nothing to chance. Having developed a dish they are happy with (which can on occasion take multiple tests), different members of the team will try the recipe in different kitchens to check that it works correctly. They also test each dish for fail-safe instructions on how you can get ahead, freeze ahead and best store it, too.

In terms of timing, it's worth noting that we take care to help you prepare dishes efficiently and multi-task. So, while you're frying an onion, for instance, we think it's possible for you to be chopping some vegetables, too – that way you'll be working according to the quickest time we estimate it takes to make a dish.

Of course, like every good mother, I love all my recipes equally! But pushed to pinpoint some favourites in this collection, I know it's the One-pan Wonders chapter I'll personally be turning to on repeat. The Mustardy Lamb Traybake is a family favourite in my house, and the Weekday Chilli has become something of a ritual when we sit down to watch *The Great British Bake Off* together. Meanwhile, I have made the Honey, Mustard and Salmon Traybake from the Just 5 Ingredients chapter so many times I think I could now do it blindfolded – and it has never once disappointed.

I wish you well in finding your own favourites in this collection, and hope we help breathe new life into your midweek meals.

Gaby

Dietary Index

Those following a vegetarian, vegan, gluten-free or dairy-free diet will find recipes throughout the cookbook where you see these symbols:

VN Vegan recipes

GF Gluten-free recipes

DF Dairy-free recipes

V Vegetarian recipes

- Check all packaging if following a specific diet, as brands vary.
- Not all cheese is vegetarian, although vegetarian cheeses (and dairy-free cheese suitable for a vegan diet) are widely available in supermarkets and health food stores. Always read the label and look out for the Vegetarian Society Approved symbol.
- Vegetable stock is not always vegan, and may contain gluten or dairy – always check the label if you are following a special diet.
- Wine may contain animal protein, so check the label to ensure it is suitable for vegetarians or vegans.

The Measurements

°C	Fan Oven	Gas mark
110	90	¼
130	110	½
140	120	1
150	130	2
170	150	3
180	160	4
190	170	5
200	180	6
220	200	7
230	210	8
240	220	9

WEIGHTS

Metric	Imperial
15g	½oz
25g	1oz
40g	1½oz
50g	2oz
75g	3oz
100g	3½oz
125g	4oz
150g	5oz
175g	6oz
200g	7oz
225g	8oz
250g	9oz
275g	10oz
300g	11oz
350g	12oz
375g	13oz
400g	14oz
425g	15oz
450g	1lb
550g	1¼lb
700g	1½lb
900g	2lb
1.1kg	2½lb

VOLUMES

Metric	Imperial
5ml	1 tsp
15ml	1 tbsp
25ml	1fl oz
50ml	2fl oz
100ml	3½fl oz
125ml	4fl oz
150ml	5fl oz (¼ pint)
175ml	6fl oz
200ml	7fl oz
250ml	9fl oz
300ml	10fl oz (½ pint)
500ml	17fl oz
600ml	1 pint
900ml	1½ pints
1 litre	1¾ pints
2 litres	3½ pints

LENGTHS

Metric	Imperial
5mm	¼in
1cm	½in
2cm	¾in
2.5cm	1in
3cm	1¼in
4cm	1½in
5cm	2in
7.5cm	3in
10cm	4in
15cm	6in
18cm	7in
20.5cm	8in
23cm	9in
25.5cm	10in
28cm	11in
30.5cm	12in

ALWAYS REMEMBER

- Use one set of measurements – never mix metric and imperial.
- Ovens and grills must be preheated to the specified temperature before cooking.
- All spoon measures are for calibrated measuring spoons and should be level, unless otherwise stated.
- Eggs are medium and free-range and butter is salted, unless otherwise stated.
- Buy the best-quality meat you can afford.

1

Midweek
Cheats

Waffle-topped Cottage Pie

**This recipe couldn't be simpler and relies on speedy shortcuts
– using potato waffles instead of mash – for a fuss-free supper.**

1 tbsp vegetable oil
1 large onion, finely chopped
400g beef mince, 5% fat
45g sachet cottage or shepherd's pie seasoning mix
250g mix frozen carrots and peas
16 mini potato waffles (see GH TIP)

Hands-on time: 15 minutes
Cooking time: about 55 minutes
Serves 4

PER SERVING 335cals, 26g protein, 13g fat
(3g saturates), 26g carbs (6g total sugars), 5g fibre

1. Preheat oven to 200°C (180°C fan) mark 6. Heat the oil in a large, deep frying pan over medium heat and fry the onion and beef for 10 minutes, stirring frequently to break up any large beef lumps, or until the onion has softened and the beef is browned.

2. Add the sachet seasoning and 400ml water. Bring to the boil and simmer for 5 minutes. Stir in the frozen carrots and peas and cook to defrost. Tip into an ovenproof serving dish. Top with the waffles, overlapping them slightly.

3. Cook in the oven for 30–35 minutes, or until the waffles are golden. Serve with seasonal greens, if you like.

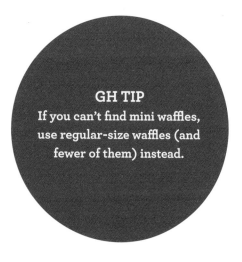

GH TIP
If you can't find mini waffles,
use regular-size waffles (and
fewer of them) instead.

Traybake
Roast Dinner

All the flavours of a Sunday roast without any of the faff.
Swap the carrots for parsnips, if you fancy.

3 tbsp vegetable oil
4 shallots, peeled and halved
2 large carrots, roughly chopped
500g pack fresh gnocchi
400g broccoli florets
250ml chicken stock
1kg mixed skin-on chicken thighs and drumsticks
150g raw cocktail sausages

Hands-on time: 20 minutes
Cooking time: about 1 hour
Serves 4

PER SERVING 895cals, 62g protein, 48g fat
(12g saturates), 48g carbs (7g total sugars), 11g fibre

1. Preheat oven to 220°C (200°C fan) mark 7. Heat 2 tablespoons oil in a large roasting tin in the oven for 10 minutes. Add the shallots and carrots to the hot oil and stir to coat. Roast for about 15 minutes, or until they have started to soften.

2. Remove the tin from the oven and stir in the gnocchi, broccoli, stock and plenty of seasoning. Arrange the chicken, skin-side up, and sausages on top of the mixture and brush with the remaining oil. Season and return to the oven for 35 minutes, until the chicken is cooked through.

Baked Red Pesto Cod with Crushed Peas

Jarred pesto works better than fresh here, as it holds its shape. You can, of course, use green rather than red pesto, if you prefer.

2 x 540g tins new potatoes in water, drained
 (650g drained weight)
1½ tbsp olive oil
4 skinless cod fillets
4 tbsp red pesto
25g panko breadcrumbs
250g frozen peas
50g butter
1 tbsp lemon juice

Hands-on time: 20 minutes
Cooking time: about 20 minutes
Serves 4

PER SERVING 482cals, 34g protein, 21g fat
(9g saturates), 35g carbs (4g total sugars), 5g fibre

1. Preheat oven to 200°C (180°C fan) mark 6. In a medium roasting tin, toss the potatoes with 1 tablespoon oil and plenty of seasoning. Lay the cod fillets on top and spread over the pesto.

2. In a small bowl, mix the breadcrumbs with the remaining half a tablespoon oil and plenty of seasoning. Sprinkle over the fish and pesto. Cook for 18–20 minutes, or until the breadcrumbs are golden and the fish is cooked through.

3. Meanwhile, heat the peas and butter in a medium pan over a medium heat, stirring until piping hot. Stir in the lemon juice and plenty of seasoning. Remove from the heat and roughly mash, using a potato masher or fork.

4. Serve the fish and potatoes with the crushed peas alongside.

Baked Thai Green Trout

You can use salmon or any white fish fillets you like instead of the trout. Blending the coconut milk with the curry paste and herbs helps the sauce come together and gives the dish an appetising bright green colour.

DF

2 x 250g pouches microwave basmati rice
4 trout fillets, skin removed if you prefer
100g baby corn, halved lengthways
100g sugar snap peas, halved lengthways
400ml tin light coconut milk
4 tbsp Thai green curry paste
Large handful coriander, stalks and leaves
1 lime, finely sliced

Hands-on time: 15 minutes
Cooking time: about 20 minutes
Serves 4

PER SERVING 557cals, 32g protein, 23g fat
(9g saturates), 55g carbs (3g total sugars), 3g fibre

1. Preheat oven to 200°C (180°C fan) mark 6. Empty the rice into a rough 2 litre ovenproof serving dish, breaking up any large lumps and spreading it out to an even layer. Arrange the fish and vegetables on top of the rice.

2. In a blender, whizz the coconut milk, curry paste, coriander and some seasoning until smooth. Pour all over the fish, vegetables and rice. Arrange the lime slices on top of the fish.

3. Cook for 15–17 minutes, or until the fish is cooked through.

Gyoza Broth

This super-easy broth is the perfect healthy, restorative supper.

1 tsp olive oil
3 garlic cloves, crushed
5cm piece fresh root ginger, peeled and finely grated
6 spring onions, finely chopped
1 litre vegetable stock
2 tbsp soy sauce (check it's vegan)
1 tsp Chinese chilli oil
100g frozen edamame beans
20 vegan gyoza
300g vegan thick udon noodles, cooked
100g baby spinach, roughly chopped

Hands-on time: 10 minutes
Cooking time: about 10 minutes
Serves 4

PER SERVING 283cals, 14g protein, 6g fat
(1g saturates), 41g carbs (7g total sugars), 6g fibre

1. Heat the oil in a large pan over medium heat. Add the garlic, ginger and most of the spring onions and cook for 1 minute, until fragrant. Add the stock, soy sauce, chilli oil and edamame and bring to the boil. Simmer for 4 minutes.

2. Add the gyoza, udon noodles and spinach and cook for 4 minutes, or until the gyoza and noodles are tender. Divide among 4 bowls and scatter over the remaining spring onions.

Sausage Fajita Pilau

This easy pilau all cooks together and makes for
a colourful and balanced meal.

2 tbsp olive oil
1 red onion, cut into 16 wedges
2 mixed colour peppers, deseeded and sliced
8 chipolata sausages, cut into rough 2cm pieces
35g fajita seasoning mix
2 x 250g pouches microwave basmati rice
200ml chicken stock
Finely grated zest 1 lime and juice ½ lime
Small handful coriander, roughly torn
Guacamole, to serve (optional)

Hands-on time: 10 minutes
Cooking time: about 30 minutes
Serves 4

**PER SERVING (without guacamole) 420cals,
14g protein, 22g fat (7g saturates), 40g carbs
(6g total sugars), 4g fibre**

1. Preheat oven to 220°C (200°C fan) mark 7.
   In a rough 2 litre ovenproof serving dish, mix
   the oil, onion, peppers and sausages with some
   salt and pepper. Cook for 15 minutes, or until
   the sausages are golden and the vegetables have
   softened. Stir through the fajita seasoning and
   return to the oven for 5 minutes.

2. Remove from the oven and stir through the rice,
   breaking up any lumps, then the stock, lime zest
   and juice. Cook for 10 minutes, or until the
   sausages are cooked through.

3. Garnish with the coriander and serve with
   guacamole, if you like.

Florentine Pizzettes

We've used 4 individual oval flatbreads, but you could
use 2 larger ones instead and halve them to serve.

Oil, to grease
200g baby spinach
150g cream cheese
4 individual garlic flatbreads
4 medium eggs
125g mozzarella ball, drained and torn

Hands-on time: 15 minutes
Cooking time: about 20 minutes
Serves 4

PER SERVING 564cals, 26g protein, 31g fat
(13g saturates), 44g carbs (7g total sugars), 3g fibre

1. Preheat oven to 200°C (180°C fan) mark 6 and
   grease or line a large baking tray with baking
   parchment. Put the spinach into a large
   heatproof bowl, then cover with just-boiled water
   from the kettle. Leave for 1 minute, then drain
   and cool under cold running water. Drain again.
   Lift up handfuls of the spinach and squeeze out
   as much excess liquid as you can. Roughly chop,
   then return to the bowl and mix in the cream
   cheese and plenty of seasoning.

2. Arrange the flatbreads on the baking tray and
   spread over the spinach mixture, leaving a small
   border around the edges. Make a well in the
   spinach mixture in the centre of each flatbread
   using the back of a spoon. Carefully crack the
   eggs into the wells. Scatter over the mozzarella
   and some freshly ground black pepper.

3. Cook for 20 minutes, or until the egg whites
   are set. Serve with a green salad, if you like.

Salted Caramel, Miso and Chocolate Tart

It doesn't get more indulgent than this easy, oozy chocolate tart.

50g unsalted butter
125g dark chocolate (70% cocoa solids), chopped
2 tbsp double cream, plus extra to serve (optional)
300g tinned caramel
1½ tbsp white miso paste
¼ tsp flaked sea salt, plus extra to sprinkle
215g sweet shortcrust pastry case

**Hands-on time: 10 minutes, plus cooling
    and 1 hour setting**
Cooking time: about 10 minutes
Serves 6–8

**PER SERVING (if serving 8) 381cals, 3g protein, 21g fat
(13g saturates), 46g carbs (35g total sugars), 1g fibre**

1. Put the butter and chocolate in a medium heatproof bowl and set over a pan of barely simmering water. Leave to melt, stirring occasionally, until smooth. Remove from the heat and stir in the cream. Set aside to cool.

2. Meanwhile, in a medium bowl, mix the caramel, miso and sea salt until combined.

3. Put the pastry case on to a serving plate. Scrape the caramel mixture into the pastry case and gently smooth to level. Scrape the slightly cooled chocolate mixture on to the caramel and smooth to level. Chill for 1 hour, until the chocolate has set.

4. Sprinkle over a little more sea salt, if you like, and serve in slices.

GET AHEAD
Make the tart up to
2 days ahead and store
in the fridge.

30-minute Rice Pudding

This speedy pudding can be served warm, chilled or at room temperature. Store any leftovers in the fridge, covered, for up to 3 days.

FOR THE RICE PUDDING
150g condensed milk
1 tbsp vanilla bean paste
500ml milk
2 x 250g pouches microwave basmati rice

FOR THE RASPBERRY COULIS
200g raspberries
2 tbsp icing sugar

Hands-on time: 15 minutes
Cooking time: about 15 minutes
Serves 6

PER SERVING 306cals, 8g protein, 7g fat (4g saturates), 52g carbs (23g total sugars), 2g fibre

1. For the rice pudding, in a large pan, mix the condensed milk, vanilla bean paste and milk. Add the rice, breaking up any clumps. Put over a medium-high heat and cook, stirring regularly, for 15 minutes, or until the rice is tender and most of the liquid has been absorbed.

2. Meanwhile, make the raspberry coulis. Whizz the raspberries and icing sugar in a blender until smooth. Pass through a fine sieve, working the pulp well (discard the seeds).

3. Divide the rice pudding among 6 bowls and serve with a drizzle of coulis.

Microwave Sticky Toffee Pudding

With this clever microwave recipe, you're only minutes away from this family favourite. Stir a pinch of flaked sea salt through your toffee sauce, if you like.

100g unsalted butter, melted, plus extra to grease
75g pitted Medjool dates
75g dark brown soft sugar
2 medium eggs, beaten
100ml milk
1 tbsp vanilla bean paste
200g sticky toffee sauce, plus extra to serve (optional)
150g self-raising flour

Hands-on time: 15 minutes, plus cooling
Cooking time: about 10 minutes
Serves 4

PER SERVING 741cals, 6g protein, 40g fat
(25g saturates), 90g carbs (61g total sugars), 2g fibre

1. Lightly grease a 2 litre (15 x 20cm) microwave-safe dish with butter. Put the dates and 100ml just-boiled water into the small bowl of a food processor and carefully pulse to a chunky purée. Alternatively, finely chop the dates and put into a small heatproof bowl with the water and leave to soak for 10 minutes.

2. In a large bowl, whisk the butter, sugar, eggs, milk, vanilla and date purée/chopped date mixture with 75g sticky toffee sauce. Whisk in the flour and a pinch of salt until combined, then scrape into the greased dish. Tightly cover with microwave-safe clingfilm and cook on full power (750W) for 4–5 minutes, until the sponge has stopped rising and is mostly firm to the touch (a small sticky patch in the centre is fine).

3. Spoon over the remaining 125g toffee sauce, re-cover with the clingfilm, and cook at the same power for 30 seconds. Leave to cool, covered, for 10 minutes, then serve with extra sauce and vanilla ice cream, if you like.

Lemon and Blueberry Cheesecake Pots

Whip up these delicious mini cheesecakes in just 15 minutes. For extra zing, you could add the finely grated zest of half a lemon to the cream cheese mixture.

125g digestive biscuits
75g butter, melted
350g cream cheese
5 tbsp icing sugar, sifted
200ml double cream
6 tbsp lemon curd
150g blueberries

Hands-on time: 15 minutes
Makes 6 pots

PER POT 606cals, 5g protein, 48g fat (29g saturates), 38g carbs (28g total sugars), 1g fibre

1. Whizz the biscuits in a food processor until finely crushed (alternatively, bash in a food bag with a rolling pin). Add the melted butter and pulse/mix until combined. Divide among 6 small tumblers or ramekins and press the surface gently to level with the back of a spoon. Chill for 5 minutes.

2. Meanwhile, in a medium bowl, mix the cream cheese and icing sugar until smooth. In a separate bowl, whisk the double cream until it holds soft peaks, then fold the cream into the cream cheese mixture using a large metal spoon.

3. Spoon 1 tablespoon lemon curd into each glass/ramekin, followed by a sprinkling of blueberries (reserve some to decorate). Divide the cream cheese mixture between the glasses/ramekins and top with the reserved blueberries to serve.

GET AHEAD
The cheesecake pots will keep for 1 day, covered and chilled.

2

One-pan Wonders

Mustardy Lamb Traybake

A luxurious yet speedy traybake. If you don't have dried mint, replace it with any dried green herb you like.

1 tbsp olive oil
1 large courgette, trimmed and cut into
  rough 1.5cm pieces
2 tbsp wholegrain mustard
12 lamb cutlets
2 x 400g tins haricot beans, drained and rinsed
150ml chicken stock
25g Parmesan, finely grated
1 tsp dried mint
250g cherry tomatoes on the vine, snipped into
  smaller portions

Hands-on time: 15 minutes
Cooking time: about 25 minutes
Serves 4

PER SERVING 455cals, 44g protein, 19g fat
(7g saturates), 22g carbs (4g total sugars), 12g fibre

1. Preheat oven to 220°C (200°C fan) mark 7. In a large ovenproof serving dish or roasting tin, mix the oil, courgette pieces and plenty of seasoning. Roast for 10 minutes.

2. Meanwhile, brush the mustard all over the cutlets.

3. Carefully remove the dish/tin from the oven and mix in the beans, stock, Parmesan and mint. Top with the lamb cutlets and return to the oven for 10 minutes.

4. Add the cherry tomatoes (still on the vine) to the tin and return to the oven for 3–5 minutes, until they are just bursting. Serve with some crusty bread, if you like.

Cajun Chicken Pasta

The key to this easy recipe is in the spice blend. You can use 1 tablespoon bought Cajun spice seasoning if short on time. Chicken breast would also work here, though chicken thighs remain juicier and more tender.

DF

FOR THE CAJUN CHICKEN
1 tsp smoked sweet paprika
½ tsp freshly ground black pepper
½ tsp cayenne pepper
¼ tsp garlic granules
1 tsp onion granules
1 tsp dried oregano
½ tsp dried thyme
300g chicken thigh fillets, cut into finger-size strips

FOR THE PASTA
1 tbsp vegetable oil
1 onion, finely chopped
400g tin chopped tomatoes
800ml chicken stock
300g conchiglie

TO SERVE
3 spring onions, finely sliced
150g guacamole (optional)

Hands-on time: 15 minutes
Cooking time: about 35 minutes
Serves 4

PER SERVING (without guacamole) 441cals, 32g protein, 6g fat (1g saturates), 62g carbs (9g total sugars), 5g fibre

1. For the Cajun chicken, in a medium bowl mix all the spices, garlic and onion granules, the dried herbs and a large pinch of salt. Add the chicken and mix to coat.

2. For the pasta, heat the oil in a large pan over low heat and cook the onion for 5 minutes, until softened. Increase the heat to medium, add the spiced chicken and cook for 5 minutes, until starting to turn golden.

3. Add the tomatoes and stock. Bring to the boil, then stir in the pasta. Bubble for 17–20 minutes, stirring frequently, or until the pasta is cooked al dente and most of the liquid has been absorbed. Check the seasoning.

4. Garnish with spring onions and serve with a dollop of guacamole, if using.

Smoked Haddock and Pea Risotto

You can choose dyed or natural smoked haddock for this recipe, as you prefer. Smoked haddock imparts a lot of flavour, and when buying it frozen, remains cost-effective. You can also use fresh haddock, if you like – the cooking time will be faster. If you have any grated Parmesan, add some with the cream cheese for a richer flavour.

1 glug oil (vegetable, olive or sunflower are best)
1 onion, finely chopped
2 garlic cloves, crushed
2 heaped tbsp risotto rice
2 fish, vegetable or chicken stock cubes
2 frozen smoked haddock fillets
¾ standard mugful frozen peas
2 heaped spoonfuls cream cheese

Hands-on time: 15 minutes
Cooking time: about 30 minutes
Serves 4

PER SERVING 415cals, 19g protein, 9g fat
(3g saturates), 63g carbs (4g total sugars), 4g fibre

1. Heat the oil in a large pan over a medium heat for 1 minute. Add the chopped onion, garlic and rice and fry, stirring constantly, for 2 minutes.

2. Crumble the stock cubes into the pan and add 2 mugfuls of just-boiled water from the kettle. Cook, stirring occasionally, for 5 minutes.

3. Add another 2 mugfuls of just-boiled water and continue to cook, stirring occasionally, for 10 minutes. Add the frozen smoked haddock fillets, making sure they are submerged in the rice mixture. Cook for 8–10 minutes, stirring occasionally, or until the rice is tender, has absorbed most of the liquid and the fish is flaked and cooked.

4. Add the peas and cream cheese and mix to heat through. Check the seasoning and serve.

Greek Salad and Meatball Traybake

If you prefer, you can use beef instead of lamb mince for this meatball dish that's brimming with Mediterranean flavours.

2 red onions, each cut into 12 wedges
1 courgette, trimmed and sliced
200g cherry tomatoes, halved if large
50g pitted black olives
400g tin butterbeans, drained and rinsed
3 garlic cloves, crushed
1 tbsp dried oregano
2 tbsp extra virgin olive oil
250g lamb mince
½ tsp ground cumin
150g crusty bread, cut into rough 2cm pieces
100g feta, crumbled
Small handful mint, leaves picked and roughly chopped

Hands-on time: 15 minutes
Cooking time: about 30 minutes
Serves 4

PER SERVING 471cals, 26g protein, 23g fat
(9g saturates), 35g carbs (9g total sugars), 9g fibre

1. Preheat oven to 200°C (180°C fan) mark 6. In a large ovenproof serving dish or shallow roasting tin, mix the onions, courgette, tomatoes, olives and butterbeans. In a small bowl, mix two-thirds of the garlic, the oregano, oil and some seasoning. Drizzle the mixture into the dish/tin and toss gently to coat. Roast for 10 minutes, or until the veg is starting to soften.

2. Meanwhile, in a separate bowl mix the lamb mince, cumin, remaining garlic and some seasoning. Shape into 12 balls. Carefully remove the dish/tin from the oven and stir in the bread pieces. Top with the meatballs and return to the oven for 20 minutes, or until the meatballs are cooked through and the veg is tender.

3. Scatter the crumbled feta and chopped mint evenly over the traybake and serve.

One-pot Chicken Pilau

Shawarma spice (sometimes called Middle Eastern spice mix) is a blend that usually includes black pepper, coriander, cinnamon, cardamom and allspice, and it makes a deliciously fragrant base for this simple pilau.

DF

1½ tbsp olive oil
1 onion, finely chopped
6 skinless chicken thigh fillets, cut
   into bite-size pieces
2 tbsp shawarma spice (see intro)
250g white basmati rice
500ml hot chicken stock
150g green beans, trimmed and cut into
   rough 2.5cm lengths
Juice 1 lemon
50g pomegranate seeds
Handful parsley, roughly chopped
2 tbsp flaked almonds (optional)

Hands-on time: 25 minutes
Cooking time: about 30 minutes
Serves 4

PER SERVING 470cals, 32g protein, 12g fat
(2g saturates), 56g carbs (5g total sugars), 3g fibre

1. Heat the oil in a large pan (that has a lid) over a medium heat and fry the onion and a large pinch of salt for 3 minutes, until beginning to soften. Add the chicken and fry for 3–4 minutes, stirring occasionally, until browned. Stir in the shawarma spice and fry for 1 minute.

2. Stir in the rice, followed by the stock. Bring to the boil, then add the beans. Cover, reduce the heat to low and cook for 12–15 minutes, until the rice is tender.

3. Add the lemon juice, pomegranate seeds and parsley, and gently mix with a fork. Check the seasoning. Scatter over the almonds, if using, and serve.

Okonomiyaki-inspired Traybake

This combines the flavours of the Japanese street-food dish
– a savoury cabbage pancake with a variety of toppings – and
the method of a toad-in-the-hole. Top it with sushi ginger
and mayo, if you like.

FOR THE BAKE
2 tbsp sesame oil (or use vegetable oil)
200g plain flour
4 large eggs
½ white cabbage, core removed and finely shredded
50g Cheddar, coarsely grated
1 tbsp soy sauce
8 spring onions, finely sliced

FOR THE SAUCE
2 tbsp ketchup
1 tsp runny honey
1 tsp soy sauce

Hands-on time: 15 minutes, plus cooling
Cooking time: about 35 minutes
Serves 4

PER SERVING 435cals, 19g protein, 17g fat
(6g saturates), 49g carbs (10g total sugars), 6g fibre

1. Preheat oven to 220°C (200°C fan) mark 7. For
   the bake, pour the oil into a roughly 25 x 30cm
   non-stick roasting tin and put into the oven to
   preheat for 5 minutes.

2. Meanwhile, in a large bowl mix the flour and a
   pinch of salt. Make a well in the centre, add the
   eggs and stir gently to combine, adding 150ml
   water to create a smooth batter.

3. Mix in the cabbage, Cheddar, soy and most of
   the spring onions. Add the mixture to the hot tin
   and spread out to level. Return to the oven for
   30 minutes, or until golden and cooked through.

4. Meanwhile, in a small bowl mix all the sauce
   ingredients until combined. Set aside.

5. Remove the tin from the oven and leave to
   cool for 5 minutes. Sprinkle over the remaining
   spring onions, drizzle over the sauce and serve.

Weekday Chilli

You can replace the beef mince with Quorn for a vegetarian version. Up the chilli flakes if you like it spicy!

1 glug oil (vegetable, olive or sunflower are best)
1 onion, finely chopped
400g pack beef mince (see intro)
½–1 teaspoon dried chilli flakes, to taste
1 red, orange or yellow pepper, deseeded and sliced
400g tin chopped tomatoes
2 tbsp tomato purée
1 standard mugful white long grain rice (not 'easy cook')
400g tin kidney beans, drained and rinsed in a sieve
    under cold water

TO SERVE (optional)
Handful tortilla chips
Handful grated Cheddar
Guacamole

Hands-on time: 15 minutes
Cooking time: about 35 minutes
Serves 4

PER SERVING (without optional ingredients) 613cals, 31g protein, 20g fat (8g saturates), 73g carbs (8g total sugars), 9g fibre

1. Heat the oil in a large pan (non-stick is ideal) over medium heat for 1 minute. Add the onion and fry, stirring occasionally, for 5 minutes. Tip in the beef mince and stir to break up any large lumps and brown the meat.

2. Add the chilli flakes, pepper, chopped tomatoes, tomato purée, then season. Bring to a bubble.

3. Add the rice to the pan, along with 5 standard mugfuls water. Bring to the boil and bubble for 15 minutes, stirring frequently to stop the rice from sticking, or until the rice is tender and has absorbed most of the liquid. Stir in the kidney beans and check the seasoning. You can serve it now, or carry on to finish the dish.

4. Preheat oven to as high as it will go or preheat grill to high. If your pan isn't ovenproof, tip the chilli into an oven-safe serving dish. Crunch over the tortilla chips and scatter over the cheese. Cook in the oven/under the grill until the cheese is melted and golden. Serve with guacamole, if you like.

Cherry Tomato
and Pesto Pasta

This all-in-one method is so easy and saves on washing-up.
Add in any extra flavours you fancy (or have in the cupboard
or fridge). Dried mixed herbs, tinned tuna and olives would
all make tasty additions.

1 glug oil (vegetable, olive or sunflower are best)
2 garlic cloves, finely chopped
2 large handfuls cherry tomatoes, halved
1 vegetable stock cube
150g spaghetti
Handful spinach leaves, roughly sliced
2 tbsp pesto

Hands-on time: 10 minutes
Cooking time: about 20 minutes
Serves 2

PER SERVING 409cals, 12g protein, 13g fat
(1g saturates), 59g carbs (5g total sugars), 6g fibre

1. Heat the oil in a large pan over medium heat
   for 1 minute. Add the garlic and halved cherry
   tomatoes and fry for 1 minute.

2. Crumble in the stock cube and add 2 standard
   mugfuls of just-boiled water from the kettle.
   When bubbling, add the pasta. As soon as you
   can without snapping it, carefully push the pasta
   down into the liquid. Once the pasta is
   submerged, cook for 10–15 minutes (depending
   on the size of your pan), stirring regularly, until
   the pasta is tender and the sauce has thickened
   and reduced.

3. Stir in the spinach until it wilts and check the
   seasoning. Swirl through the pesto and divide
   between 2 bowls to serve.

One-pot Mexican-style Quinoa

This healthy hands-off dish is on the table in 30 minutes and only uses one pan! If you have leftovers, roll them up in tortilla wraps and bake like enchiladas.

200g quinoa, rinsed
2 large tomatoes, roughly chopped
2 red onions, finely chopped
1 tsp ground cumin
1 tsp smoked paprika
1 tsp mild chilli powder
1 red pepper, deseeded and finely chopped
400g tin black beans, drained and rinsed
340g tin sweetcorn, drained and rinsed
2 avocados, destoned and finely chopped
Juice 2 limes
Large handful coriander, finely chopped

Hands-on time: 10 minutes
Cooking time: about 30 minutes
Serves 4

PER SERVING 481cals, 16g protein, 19g fat
(4g saturates), 54g carbs (16g total sugars), 16g fibre

1. In a large pan (that has a lid) mix the quinoa, tomatoes, red onions, spices, plenty of seasoning and 400ml water. Cover and bring to the boil over high heat, then turn down the heat and simmer for 25 minutes, adding the pepper, beans and sweetcorn for the final 3 minutes, or until the quinoa is tender and has absorbed the water.

2. Stir in the chopped avocados, lime juice and coriander. Check the seasoning and serve.

Speedy Sausage Stew

Quick, comforting and full of seasonal veg, this quick stew is exactly what we're craving in colder weather. The best bit? It requires just a few simple ingredients and is on the table in 30 minutes. Serve as is or with steamed greens and a dollop of fiery French mustard.

8 Toulouse sausages
2 tbsp oil
2 red onions, sliced
2 garlic cloves, chopped
3 thyme sprigs
2 x 250g packs ready-to-eat Puy lentils (see GH TIP)
300ml chicken stock
3 tbsp balsamic vinegar
150g kale

Hands-on time: 5 minutes
Cooking time: about 25 minutes
Serves 4

PER SERVING 632cals, 44g protein, 32g fat
(10g saturates), 41g carbs (10g total sugars), 4g fibre

1. In a large frying pan over high heat, brown the sausages in half the oil for 3 minutes. Remove to a plate.

2. Add the remaining oil to the pan with the onions and fry, covered, over a low heat for 10 minutes until softened and lightly browned. Add the garlic and thyme, stirring for 1 minute.

3. Return the sausages to the pan, then add the lentils, stock and vinegar. Cover and simmer for 10 minutes. Stir in the kale to wilt for 1 minute and serve.

GH TIP
We used a packet of ready-to-eat Puy lentils, but you could use a 400g tin of cooked brown lentils.

3

Better than
a Takeaway

Frying-pan Pizza

Yogurt and self-raising flour make this a super-speedy and deliciously fluffy pizza base. If you prefer it crispy, roll the dough out thinner.

1 standard mugful self-raising flour, plus extra to dust
6 heaped tbsp Greek-style yogurt
2½–3 heaped tbsp tomato purée, as needed
½ x 125g mozzarella ball, torn into smaller pieces
10 pepperoni slices
Few basil leaves, to serve (optional)

Hands-on time: 20 minutes
Cooking time: about 10 minutes
Makes 1 pizza (serves 1–2)

PER HALF PIZZA 660cals, 30g protein, 23g fat
(12g saturates), 82g carbs (6g total sugars), 5g fibre

1. In a medium bowl, mix the flour, a pinch of fine salt and the yogurt to make a dough. Tip on to a lightly floured work surface and knead to bring together. Shape into a ball.

2. Preheat grill to high (see GH TIP). Flour your work surface again, if needed, then press out the dough with your fingers or roll out with a rolling pin or bottle to a rough 25cm round (or the size of the base of a large, ovenproof frying pan).

3. Heat the large ovenproof frying pan (ideally one that has a lid) over medium-high heat for 1 minute. Add the dough round and fry, covered with the lid or a large baking tray, for 2–3 minutes, or until the base is speckled golden. Flip the dough and spread the tomato purée on top, leaving a rough 1.5cm border. Scatter over the mozzarella and pepperoni and put under the grill for 3 minutes, or until the cheese is melted and bubbling.

4. Transfer the pizza to a plate or board and scatter over the basil, if using. Serve in slices.

GH TIP
If you don't have a grill, you can cook the pizza through on the hob, either covered with the lid or a large baking tray to help melt the cheese.

Oyster Mushroom Shawarma

Traditionally, a shawarma consists of layers of meat cooked on a spit. We've fried the oyster mushrooms here before layering on sticks to give them extra flavour and texture. The marinade enhances their delicious umami taste.

600g oyster mushrooms
2 tbsp olive oil
2 tbsp rose harissa paste
2 tbsp soy sauce
1 tsp ground cumin

YOU WILL ALSO NEED
4 wooden skewers, soaked in water for 30 minutes

Hands-on time: 15 minutes
Cooking time: about 25 minutes
Makes 4 skewers

PER SKEWER 80cals, 4g protein, 6g fat (1g saturates), 2g carbs (2g total sugars), 0g fibre

GH TIP
The first stage of this recipe is fairly time-consuming – speed it up by frying the mushrooms in 2 large pans, if possible.

1. Leave most of the mushrooms whole, but tear in half if large. Heat a large frying pan (see GH TIP) over high heat and add half a tablespoon of oil. Cook the mushrooms in batches for 2–3 minutes per side, or until golden. To extract extra moisture, place a heavy pan on top while they are frying.

2. Transfer to a baking tray lined with kitchen paper while you repeat the process with the remaining mushrooms, adding the remaining 1½ tablespoons oil as needed.

3. In a small bowl, mix the harissa, soy sauce, cumin and some seasoning.

4. Divide the mushrooms among the skewers and return to the baking tray (without the kitchen paper). Brush over all the harissa mixture.

5. Griddle or barbecue over medium heat for 10 minutes, turning regularly, until charred. Alternatively, char in an oven preheated to 200°C (180°C fan) mark 6 for 15 minutes, turning halfway. If you'd like to serve with a dip, we made garlic yogurt (see page 60) with added lemon zest.

Chicken Chow Mein

Boost the colour and flavour of this delicious stir-fry by adding any other crisp seasonal vegetables you like along with the red peppers.

200g medium egg noodles
1 tsp sesame oil
400g skinless chicken breasts
1½ tsp Chinese five spice
1 tbsp vegetable oil
2 red peppers, deseeded and sliced
5 spring onions, thinly sliced
Large handful beansprouts

FOR THE SAUCE
2.5cm piece fresh root ginger, peeled and grated
2 garlic cloves, crushed
1 tbsp cornflour
1½ tbsp oyster sauce
1½ tbsp tomato ketchup
2 tbsp light soy sauce

Hands-on time: 15 minutes
Cooking time: about 15 minutes
Serves 4

PER SERVING 377cals, 31g protein, 7g fat (1g saturates), 46g carbs (7g total sugars), 5g fibre

1. Make the sauce. In a small bowl, mix together the ginger, garlic and cornflour. Whisk in the remaining sauce ingredients and set aside.

2. Bring a medium pan of water to the boil and cook the noodles according to the pack instructions. Drain well, then toss through the sesame oil to stop them from sticking together and set aside.

3. Cut the chicken into finger-size strips and put into a large bowl. Add the Chinese five spice and some seasoning and toss together.

4. Heat the vegetable oil in a large wok until smoking hot. Add the chicken and stir-fry over high heat for 5 minutes until golden and cooked through – if you find the chicken is sticking, add a splash of water. Add the peppers, spring onions and beansprouts and cook for 1–2 minutes until just softened. Stir in the noodles and sauce to heat through in the wok. Check the seasoning and serve.

Lamb Shish Kebab

This takeaway favourite is so quick and simple to whip up at home. Drizzling the lamb with sweet and sharp pomegranate molasses adds an authentic Turkish finish that's quite addictive.

4 lamb leg steaks (400g total), cut into large, even chunks
3 garlic cloves, crushed
2 tsp dried oregano
Finely grated zest 1 lemon
2 tbsp olive oil

FOR THE GARLIC YOGURT
100g natural yogurt
2 garlic cloves, crushed
1 tbsp lemon juice

TO SERVE
4 folded flatbreads or pitta breads
Mixed salad (we used crunchy lettuce, tomatoes and cucumber)
Pomegranate molasses
Chilli sauce (optional)

YOU WILL ALSO NEED
4 skewers, soaked in cold water for 20 minutes if wooden

Hands-on time: 15 minutes
Cooking time: about 10 minutes
Serves 4

PER SERVING (without salad, molasses or chilli sauce)
354cals, 23g protein, 20g fat (7g saturates), 20g carbs
(3g total sugars), 1g fibre

1. Preheat grill to high. Mix the lamb, garlic, oregano, lemon zest, olive oil and plenty of seasoning in a bowl.

2. Thread the lamb on to 4 skewers, put on a baking tray and grill for 8–10 minutes, turning once, until cooked through.

3. Meanwhile, in a small bowl, whisk the garlic yogurt ingredients with some seasoning.

4. To serve, toast the flatbreads (cut in half if using a pitta, to make pockets). Top or fill each bread with salad and a lamb skewer, then drizzle with pomegranate molasses, the garlic yogurt and chilli sauce, if using. Serve.

GH TIP
If you are not a fan of lamb, use chicken thigh fillets instead. Grill until the meat is cooked through.

Ultimate American Burger

Succulent and simple, this is the only beef burger recipe you need.

500g good-quality steak mince
½ small onion, finely chopped
1 medium egg
½ tbsp Dijon mustard
100g fresh white breadcrumbs
2 tbsp sunflower oil
8 Cheddar cheese slices
4 burger buns

TO SERVE (optional)
Little Gem lettuce leaves
Tomato slices
Gherkin spears

Hands-on time: 20 minutes, plus chilling
Cooking time: about 20 minutes
Makes 4 burgers

PER BURGER (without extras) 657cals, 50g protein,
31g fat (15g saturates), 43g carbs (3g total sugars),
3g fibre

1. Put the mince into a large bowl and mix in the chopped onion, egg, mustard, breadcrumbs and plenty of seasoning. Divide the mixture equally into 4 and shape each portion into a flattened patty. Arrange the burgers on a plate, then cover and chill for 30 minutes to firm up a little.

2. Preheat oven to 200°C (180°C fan) mark 6. Heat the oil in a large frying pan over medium–high heat and fry the burgers for 8 minutes, turning midway through, until each side is well browned. Transfer to a baking tray and lay a slice of cheese on top of each patty. Cook in the oven for 12 minutes, adding another slice of cheese to each after 6 minutes.

3. Meanwhile, toast the buns. Check to make sure the burgers are cooked through and serve in the buns, topped with lettuce leaves, tomato slices and a gherkin spear, if you like. Serve with fries and your favourite sauces.

Pork Tacos

Swap the pork mince for beef, if you like. A packet spice mix would work well here in place of the individual herbs and spices – look for ones labelled as taco or fajita seasoning.

1 tbsp olive oil
500g pork mince
2 garlic cloves, crushed
1 tbsp dried oregano
1 tbsp ground cumin
½ tbsp sweet smoked paprika
1 tsp dried chilli flakes

FOR THE SALSA
1 red onion, finely chopped
1 red chilli, deseeded and finely chopped
4 large ripe tomatoes, chopped
Juice 1 lime

TO SERVE
8 hard taco shells
125g Cheddar, coarsely grated
4 tbsp soured cream
Large handful coriander, roughly chopped

Hands-on time: 15 minutes
Cooking time: about 15 minutes
Serves 4

PER SERVING (2 filled tacos) 554cals, 35g protein, 36g fat (14g saturates), 22g carbs (6g total sugars), 3g fibre

1. In a bowl, combine all the salsa ingredients with some seasoning. Set aside. Warm the taco shells according to the pack instructions, if you like.

2. Heat the oil in a large frying pan over high heat and cook the mince, stirring to break up any clumps, until browned all over. Turn down the heat to medium, stir through the garlic, oregano, spices and some seasoning. Cook for 2 minutes. Add the salsa and cook for 2 minutes, until the tomatoes have broken down a little and the pork is cooked through.

3. Spoon the mince mixture into the taco shells and top with the Cheddar, soured cream and some chopped coriander.

Black Bean Beef

Fragrant and hearty, this classic Chinese takeaway dish is so easy
to make at home and sure to be a hit with everyone who tries it.

500g rump steak
2 tbsp vegetable oil
2 garlic cloves, sliced
2.5cm fresh ginger, finely chopped
2 tbsp black bean sauce
1 each red and yellow pepper, sliced
1 red onion, finely sliced
Large handful coriander, chopped (optional)

FOR THE MARINADE
1 tsp caster sugar
2 tsp soy sauce
2 tsp Chinese rice wine or dry sherry
1½ tsp cornflour
1 tbsp vegetable oil

Hands-on time: 15 minutes
Cooking time: about 15 minutes, plus marinating
Serves 4

1. In large bowl, mix together the marinade
   ingredients. Trim any fat from the steaks
   and slice into finger-width pieces. Add to the
   marinade, mix and set aside for 30 minutes.

2. Heat 1 tablespoon oil in a wok over high heat.
   Add the garlic, ginger and black bean sauce.
   Fry for 1 minute. Add the peppers and onion
   and fry for 2 minutes. Empty into a bowl.

3. Add the remaining oil and the beef mixture
   to the wok. Stir-fry for 3 minutes. Return the
   vegetables to the wok with 150ml water.
   Bubble for 2 minutes and check the seasoning.
   Serve with Egg-fried Rice (see below) and
   fresh coriander, if you like.

PER SERVING (without rice) 358cals, 28g protein, 21g fat (6g saturates), 12g carbs (9g total sugars), 3g fibre

Egg-fried Rice

2 eggs
1 tbsp toasted sesame oil
2 tbsp vegetable oil
2 x 250g pouches microwave rice
125g peas
4 spring onions, sliced

Hands-on time: 5 minutes
Cooking time: about 10 minutes
Serves 4

1. Whisk together the eggs and sesame oil.
   Heat the vegetable oil in a wok, then add the
   rice and fry for 3 minutes.

2. Add the peas and spring onions and cook for
   2 minutes. Push the mixture to one side of the
   wok and add the egg mix to the empty side. Cook
   until just set, then mix into the vegetable rice.

PER SERVING 300cals, 10g protein, 12g fat (2g saturates), 38g carbs (2g total sugars), 3g fibre

Chickpea and Mushroom Enchiladas

An adaptable recipe that works for brunch, lunch or dinner.
Adjust the chilli to your heat tolerance.

465g jar roasted peppers, drained
2 tsp vegetable oil
1 red onion, finely chopped
400g baby chestnut mushrooms, halved or quartered
   if large
2 tbsp chipotle paste
2 garlic cloves, crushed
400g tin chickpeas, drained and rinsed
Juice 1 lime, plus wedges to serve
Large handful coriander, roughly chopped
75g vegetarian mature Cheddar or Red Leicester, grated
8 flour tortillas
150ml soured cream

Hands-on time: 25 minutes
Cooking time: about 40 minutes
Serves 4

PER SERVING 665cals, 24g protein, 26g fat
(10g saturates), 81g carbs (10g total sugars), 5g fibre

1. Preheat oven to 200°C (180°C fan) mark 6.
Whizz 200g of the peppers in the small bowl of
a food processor, or purée using a stick blender,
until smooth. Slice the remaining peppers to
make 8 long pieces. Set aside.

2. Heat the oil in a large, deep frying pan over
low heat and fry the onion for 5 minutes, until
slightly softened. Increase the heat to medium,
add the mushrooms and fry for 5 minutes, until
golden. Stir in the chipotle paste and garlic and
cook for 1 minute. Stir in the chickpeas and
pepper purée and bubble for 1 minute,. Remove
from the heat and stir in the lime juice, half the
coriander, 25g grated cheese and some seasoning.

3. Lay a pepper strip in the middle of a tortilla,
spread one eighth of the mushroom filling on
top and roll up tightly. Repeat with the remaining
tortillas, peppers and filling. Arrange the rolls
(seam-down) in a single layer in a 2.5 litre
ovenproof dish. Spread the soured cream on
top, then scatter over the remaining cheese.

4. Cook in the oven for 25 minutes, or until golden.
Scatter over the remaining coriander and serve
with lime wedges for squeezing over.

Greek Lamb Gyros

The Greeks' answer to doner kebabs: tender lamb and
crunchy salad, all wrapped up in a toasted pitta.

450g lamb leg steaks
Large handful chopped mixed soft herbs (we used
    parsley, dill and mint), plus extra to serve
2 tbsp harissa paste
3 garlic cloves, crushed
2 tbsp olive oil
Finely grated zest and juice 1 lemon

FOR THE PICKLED ONION
1 small red onion, finely sliced
1 red chilli, deseeded and finely sliced
1 tbsp red wine vinegar
½ tsp caster sugar

TO SERVE
4 pitta breads
1 Little Gem lettuce, thickly shredded
2 tomatoes, sliced
½ cucumber, sliced
Natural yogurt, to drizzle

**Hands-on time: 30 minutes, plus marinating
    and pickling**
Cooking time: about 10 minutes
Makes 4 gyros

PER GYRO 406cals, 29g protein, 15g fat (6g saturates),
37g carbs (7g total sugars), 4g fibre

1. Put the lamb, herbs, harissa, garlic, olive oil,
   lemon zest and juice into a food bag or non-
   metallic bowl and mix to coat well. Close/cover
   and chill for at least 4 hours, or overnight.

2. In a small pan, mix the pickled onion
   ingredients and half a teaspoon salt. Heat until
   just boiling. Remove from the heat and set aside
   for 30 minutes. Cover and chill until needed.

3. Heat a griddle or frying pan over medium-high
   heat. Cook the lamb, reserving any leftover
   marinade, for 3 minutes on each side, until
   charred and pink in the centre (cook for longer
   if you prefer). Transfer to a plate to rest for a
   couple of minutes.

4. Brush one side of each pitta with any remaining
   marinade. Griddle or fry to heat through and
   soak up any extra cooking juices. Slice the lamb.
   Pile the lettuce, tomatoes, cucumber, lamb and
   pickled onion on to the pittas, then drizzle over
   some yogurt. Sprinkle with extra herbs and serve.

Prawn Pad Thai

A street-food classic, this should have a delicious mixture of hot, sour, salty and crunchy in every mouthful.

300g flat, folded dried rice noodles
3 tbsp palm or light brown soft sugar
3 tbsp tamarind paste
4 tbsp fish sauce
2 tbsp soy sauce
2 medium eggs, beaten
2 tbsp vegetable oil
3 garlic cloves, finely chopped
2 small Thai/bird's eye red chillies, chopped
300g cooked and peeled king prawns
200g beansprouts
4 spring onions, finely sliced
Small handful roasted salted peanuts, roughly chopped
Small handful coriander leaves
Lime wedges, to serve

Hands-on time: 20 minutes, plus soaking
Cooking time: about 15 minutes
Serves 4

PER SERVING 540cals, 29g protein, 13g fat
(2g saturates), 76g carbs (17g total sugars), 3g fibre

1. Put the rice noodles in large bowl and cover with just-boiled water. Leave to soak for 5 minutes, or until flexible. Drain and rinse under cold water. Meanwhile, mix the sugar, tamarind, fish sauce and soy sauce with 100ml water in a small pan. Heat gently, stirring until the sugar dissolves. Whisk 1 tablespoon of this mixture into the beaten eggs and set the sauce and eggs aside.

2. Heat the oil in a large, deep frying pan or wok over high heat. Add the garlic and chillies, stir-fry for 30 seconds, then add the drained noodles and toss briefly. Pour in the sauce and stir-fry for 2–3 minutes until the sauce is absorbed and the noodles are cooked through. Tip into a large bowl.

3. Add the egg mixture to the empty pan/wok over a medium heat and fry, stirring, until just starting to set and scramble. Return the noodle mixture to the pan, along with the prawns, beansprouts and spring onions, and stir to heat through. Serve scattered with the peanuts and coriander, with lime wedges on the side.

4

Pasta
Pronto

Four Cheese Mac 'n' Cheese

This rich mac 'n' cheese really packs a punch. For a milder flavour, swap the Camembert for Brie and leave out the Stilton. Make sure all your cheeses are vegetarian, if needed.

V

300g macaroni pasta
40g butter
40g plain flour
500ml milk
150g Camembert, rind removed and roughly chopped
75g Cheddar, coarsely grated
50g Red Leicester, coarsely grated
50g Stilton, crumbled
50g fresh white breadcrumbs

Hands-on time: 20 minutes
Cooking time: 20 minutes
Serves 4

PER SERVING 800cals, 34g protein, 38g fat
(23g saturates), 78g carbs (8g total sugars), 4g fibre

1. Bring a large pan of salted water to the boil and cook the pasta according to the pack instructions. Drain.

2. Meanwhile, melt the butter in a large pan over medium heat. Add the flour and cook, stirring, for 1 minute. Remove from the heat and gradually stir in the milk to make a smooth sauce. Return to the heat and cook, stirring, until bubbling. Season to taste.

3. Preheat grill to high. Remove the sauce from the heat and stir in the Camembert and most of the Cheddar and Red Leicester, then season well. Stir in the pasta, then empty into a roughly 2 litre ovenproof serving dish and sprinkle over the Stilton, breadcrumbs, and remaining Cheddar and Red Leicester.

4. Grill for 5 minutes, or until golden and bubbling. Serve with a salad, if you like.

Crab Linguine

An easy, elegant supper that's ready in 15 minutes. You can also use the more economical tinned crab here – just make sure to drain it thoroughly first.

DF

300g linguine pasta
1 tbsp olive oil
2 garlic cloves, finely sliced
200g mixed white and brown fresh crab meat (see GH TIP)
½ tsp dried chilli flakes
Juice 1 lemon
Large handful parsley, roughly chopped

Hands-on time: 10 minutes
Cooking time: about 15 minutes
Serves 4

PER SERVING 354cals, 19g protein, 6g fat (1g saturates), 54g carbs (2g total sugars), 4g fibre

1. Bring a large pan of salted water to the boil and cook the pasta according to the pack instructions. Drain.

2. Meanwhile, heat the oil in a large, deep frying pan over medium heat and fry the garlic for 2 minutes, until fragrant. Stir in the crab meat and chilli flakes and fry for 2 minutes.

3. Add the pasta, lemon juice, parsley and some seasoning. Toss well to combine, divide among 4 bowls and serve.

GH TIP
Brown crab meat adds great flavour, but if you prefer a more delicate taste, just use the white meat.

Smoked Salmon Pasta

If you can't find strozzapreti, fusilli or penne would work well for this recipe, too. Use a pack of flaked hot smoked salmon instead of fillets, if you prefer.

300g strozzapreti pasta
3 tbsp olive oil
75g fresh white breadcrumbs
2 garlic cloves, crushed
1 red chilli, deseeded and finely sliced
125g sun-blush tomatoes, roughly chopped
2 x hot smoked salmon fillets (about 180g), skin removed
2 tbsp nonpareille capers, drained
60g rocket

Hands-on time: 20 minutes
Cooking time: about 20 minutes
Serves 4

PER SERVING 562cals, 23g protein, 19g fat
(3g saturates), 72g carbs (6g total sugars), 6g fibre

1. Bring a large pan of salted water to the boil and cook the pasta according to the pack instructions. Drain, reserving 125ml of the cooking water.

2. Meanwhile, heat 1 tablespoon oil in a large, deep frying pan over medium heat and fry the breadcrumbs, half the garlic and plenty of seasoning, stirring regularly, until golden. Tip on to a plate and set aside.

3. Add the remaining 2 tablespoons oil to the empty pan and fry the remaining garlic, the chilli and tomatoes for 2 minutes, stirring occasionally, until fragrant. Flake in the salmon and warm through.

4. Stir in the capers, pasta, reserved cooking water and plenty of seasoning. Stir through the rocket to wilt slightly. Check the seasoning, then divide among 4 bowls and scatter over the golden breadcrumbs to serve.

Green Goat's Cheese Gnocchi

This fresh and vibrant gnocchi recipe looks impressive but comes together quickly. Swap the spinach for blanched cavolo nero, if you prefer.

750g fresh gnocchi
200g spinach
200g peas
75g vegetarian Italian-style hard cheese (or use Parmesan), finely grated
Finely grated zest 1 lemon
150ml hot vegetable stock
150g soft goat's cheese

Hands-on time: 15 minutes
Cooking time: about 15 minutes
Serves 4

PER SERVING 462cals, 20g protein, 11g fat (7g saturates), 66g carbs (3g total sugars), 8g fibre

1. Cook the gnocchi in a large pan of salted boiling water according to the pack instructions. Drain and return to the pan.

2. Meanwhile, whizz the spinach, peas, hard cheese, lemon zest, stock and plenty of seasoning in a blender until fairly smooth (you may need to stop blending and stir the mixture a couple of times to get the smoothness).

3. Add to the pan with the drained gnocchi and cook over low heat until piping hot. Check the seasoning. Divide among 4 bowls, crumble over the goat's cheese and sprinkle with freshly ground black pepper.

Pasta Primavera
with Broccoli Pesto

Inspired by the Italian soup, this is full of spring flavours. Wholewheat
pasta adds an appealing nuttiness, but white will work, too.

FOR THE PESTO
1 small head broccoli (about 300g)
50g vegetarian Italian-style hard cheese (or use
    Parmesan), grated, plus extra to serve (optional)
1 garlic clove, crushed
100g basil (stalks and leaves), roughly chopped
Small handful mint leaves
3 tbsp pine nuts
Finely grated zest and juice 1 lemon
3 tbsp extra virgin olive oil

FOR THE PASTA
300g wholewheat farfalle pasta
1 tbsp olive oil
2 spring onions, trimmed and chopped
1 courgette, trimmed and roughly chopped
75g green beans, trimmed and cut into shorter lengths
75g frozen peas

Hands-on time: 25 minutes
Cooking time: about 20 minutes
Serves 4

PER SERVING 565cals, 24g protein, 26g fat
(5g saturates), 54g carbs (6g total sugars), 11g fibre

GH TIP
Make the pesto up to 1 day
ahead, then cover and chill.
Complete the recipe from
step 4 to serve.

1. For the pesto, bring a large pan of salted water
   to the boil. Roughly chop the broccoli (including
   the stalks) and cook for 4 minutes, or until just
   tender. Using a slotted spoon, lift the broccoli
   into the bowl of a food processor (reserve the
   water for the pasta).

2. Add the remaining pesto ingredients and plenty
   of seasoning to the food processor and pulse
   until finely chopped and combined, adding
   a little cold water to loosen, if needed. Set aside.

3. For the pasta, bring the broccoli cooking water
   back up to the boil. Add the pasta and cook
   according to the pack instructions. Drain,
   reserving 175ml of the cooking water.

4. Meanwhile, heat the oil in a large, deep frying
   pan over medium heat. Cook the spring onions,
   courgette and beans for 5 minutes, stirring
   occasionally, or until starting to soften.

5. Add the pasta, peas, pesto and reserved water to
   the pan and heat, stirring regularly, until piping
   hot. Check the seasoning.

6. Divide among 4 bowls and garnish with extra
   cheese, if you like.

Creamy Sausage Pasta Bake

This Spanish-inspired bake is easy to adapt. Use a different sausage, up the chilli, swap the Manchego for Parmesan, or use any flavoured passata you like.

200g chorizo cooking sausages
½ tbsp olive oil
1 small onion, finely chopped
1 red chilli, deseeded and finely chopped
300g rigatoni pasta
2 tbsp sundried tomato purée
125ml dry white wine
500g passata with basil
75g mascarpone or crème fraîche
50g Manchego, grated

Hands-on time: 15 minutes
Cooking time: about 35 minutes
Serves 4

PER SERVING 690cals, 27g protein, 32g fat (15g saturates), 65g carbs (10g total sugars), 6g fibre

1. Remove and discard the skin from the chorizo sausages and break the meat into small pieces. Heat the oil in a large, deep frying pan over medium heat and fry the sausage pieces for 5 minutes, or until starting to turn golden.

2. Add the onion and chilli and cook, stirring occasionally, for 10–12 minutes, or until the onion is softened and golden.

3. Meanwhile, bring a large pan of salted water to the boil and cook the pasta according to pack instructions. Drain. Preheat oven to 220°C (200°C fan) mark 7.

4. Meanwhile, stir the sundried tomato purée and wine into the onion pan. Increase the heat to high and bubble for 2 minutes. Stir in the passata, bring to a simmer, then remove from the heat. Stir in the mascarpone/crème fraîche until melted, followed by the pasta. Check the seasoning.

5. Tip into a roughly 2 litre ovenproof serving dish and scatter over the Manchego. Cook in the oven for 15 minutes, or until golden and bubbling.

Fettuccine
Alfredo

Originating in Rome, this recipe was initially made with just butter and Parmesan. It's since evolved into a popular American dish with the addition of cream, and often chicken and prawns.

(V)

300g fettucine pasta
200ml double cream
75g butter, chopped
100g vegetarian Italian-style hard cheese (or use Parmesan), finely grated
25g parsley, leaves picked and finely chopped

Hands-on time: 15 minutes
Cooking time: about 15 minutes
Serves 4

PER SERVING 765cals, 19g protein, 51g fat (31g saturates), 55g carbs (3g total sugars), 4g fibre

1. Bring a large pan of salted water to the boil and cook the pasta according to pack instructions. Drain, reserving 250ml cooking water.

2. Meanwhile, heat the cream and butter in a large, deep frying pan over medium heat, stirring until the butter melts. Increase the heat to medium–high and bubble for 2 minutes, stirring occasionally, until thickened.

3. Remove the frying pan from the heat, stir in the pasta, reserved cooking water, cheese and plenty of seasoning. Toss to coat the pasta in the sauce. Check the seasoning.

4. Divide among 4 bowls and sprinkle over the parsley to serve.

GH TIP
Add a handful of shredded cooked chicken or peeled and cooked king prawns at step 3, if you like. Ensure the pasta is piping hot before serving.

Pasta alla Norma

A Sicilian favourite with great texture. It's traditionally made with spaghetti, but we've gone for a chunky tortiglioni shape here that's a joy to eat.

2 tbsp olive oil
2 aubergines, trimmed and cut into 1.5–2cm pieces
300g tortiglioni pasta
Large handful basil
2 garlic cloves, crushed
1 tbsp nonpareille capers, drained
¼–½ tsp dried chilli flakes, to taste
400g tin chopped tomatoes
1 tbsp vegetarian red wine vinegar
50g vegetarian Italian-style hard cheese (or use Pecorino Romano), finely grated

Hands-on time: 20 minutes
Cooking time: about 30 minutes
Serves 4

PER SERVING 426cals, 16g protein, 11g fat
(4g saturates), 61g carbs (8g total sugars), 8g fibre

1. Heat 1 tablespoon oil in a large, wide casserole dish or frying pan over low-medium heat. Add the aubergine and a large pinch of salt and fry, stirring occasionally, for 10–15 minutes, or until golden and tender.

2. Meanwhile, bring a large pan of salted water to the boil and cook the pasta according to the pack instructions. Drain, reserving a cupful of the cooking water.

3. Pick the basil leaves from the stems. Finely slice the stems and set the leaves aside. Add the remaining 1 tablespoon oil to the aubergine dish/pan and stir in the garlic, basil stems, capers, chilli flakes and some seasoning. Fry for 1 minute, then stir in the tomatoes and vinegar.

4. Cook over low-medium heat for 10–15 minutes, or until pulpy and thick.

5. Add the pasta and a splash of the reserved cooking water to the aubergine dish/pan. Tear in most of the basil leaves and add half the cheese. Toss to combine and check the seasoning.

6. Divide among 4 bowls and garnish with the remaining basil leaves and cheese to serve.

Baked Leek and Meatball Rigatoni

Featuring rigatoni baked into a creamy leek and tarragon
sauce, this pasta bake – which turns sausages into meatballs
– makes for a delicious meal for when you fancy something
simple yet indulgent.

300g rigatoni pasta
4 pork sausages
1 tbsp oil
2 leeks, trimmed and sliced
200ml vegetable stock
50ml double cream
200g full-fat cream cheese
1 tbsp wholegrain mustard
4 tarragon sprigs, leaves picked and chopped (see
    GH TIP)
40g Parmesan, finely grated

Hands-on time: 15 minutes
Cooking time: about 35 minutes
Serves 4

PER SERVING 590cals, 21g protein, 27g fat
(11g saturates), 62g carbs (6g total sugars), 8g fibre

GH TIP
If you can't get hold of
fresh tarragon, replace
it with 1 teaspoon dried
tarragon, dried basil
or dried mixed herbs.

1. Bring a large pan of salted water to the boil
   and cook the pasta according to the pack
   instructions. Drain.

2. Remove and discard the skin from the sausages
   and shape the meat into small balls (about
   5 from each sausage). Heat the oil in a large,
   deep frying pan over medium heat and cook the
   meatballs until well browned. Remove to a plate.

3. Preheat oven to 190°C (170°C fan) mark 5.
   Add the leeks to the empty sausage pan and
   cook, stirring occasionally, for 2–3 minutes, or
   until starting to soften. Stir in the stock and
   cream, followed by the meatballs. Increase the
   heat to high and simmer for 3 minutes.

4. Remove from the heat, stir in the cream cheese,
   mustard, tarragon and some seasoning. Add the
   pasta and mix to combine. Check the seasoning.

5. Spoon into a roughly 2 litre ovenproof serving
   dish. Sprinkle over the Parmesan and cook in
   the oven for 20 minutes, or until bubbling and
   golden. Serve with a green salad, if you like.

Miso Carbonara

Miso adds salty savouriness to this veggie carbonara. You can swap the edamame for podded broad beans or peas, if you like.

300g spaghetti
150g frozen edamame beans
3 medium eggs
100g vegetarian Italian-style hard cheese (or use Parmesan), finely grated
3 tbsp white miso paste
2 spring onions, finely sliced

Hands-on time: 15 minutes
Cooking time: about 15 minutes
Serves 4

PER SERVING 517cals, 30g protein, 16g fat (6g saturates), 61g carbs (2g total sugars), 5g fibre

1. Bring a large pan of salted water to the boil and cook the pasta according to the pack instructions, adding the edamame beans for the final 3 minutes. Drain, reserving a small cupful of the cooking water.

2. In a medium bowl, whisk the eggs, 75g cheese, the miso and plenty of freshly ground black pepper until combined.

3. Return the pasta and edamame to the pan (off the heat), then add the egg mixture and 75ml reserved cooking water. Toss to combine, adding a little more cooking water, if needed, until glossy. Warm through over low heat, if needed.

4. Divide among 4 bowls and sprinkle over the remaining cheese, the spring onions and plenty of freshly ground black pepper.

Pomodoro Tortellini Bake

A classic pomodoro sauce – made with just four basic ingredients – forms the basis of this easy and comforting recipe, which is sure to become a family favourite.

FOR THE POMODORO SAUCE
1 tbsp extra virgin olive oil
2 garlic cloves, crushed
2 x 400g tins plum tomatoes
Small handful basil, leaves picked and roughly chopped

FOR THE BAKE
500g fresh spinach and ricotta tortellini
150g mozzarella, torn
25g vegetarian Italian-style hard cheese (or use Parmesan), finely grated

Hands-on time: 15 minutes
Cooking time: about 35 minutes
Serves 4

PER SERVING 487cals, 24g protein, 23g fat (11g saturates), 44g carbs (14g total sugars), 2.3g fibre

1. For the pomodoro sauce, heat the oil in a large pan over medium heat. Add the garlic and cook for 1 minute, until fragrant. Stir in the remaining sauce ingredients and some seasoning. Bubble for 10 minutes, breaking up the tomatoes with the back of a wooden spoon, until reduced but still saucy. Check the seasoning.

2. Preheat oven to 200°C (180°C fan) mark 6. For the bake, mix the tortellini into the pomodoro sauce, then empty into a roughly 2 litre ovenproof serving dish. Make sure all the tortellini are well covered, so they won't catch in the oven.

3. Dot over the mozzarella and scatter over the hard cheese. Cook in the oven for 20 minutes, or until golden and bubbling. Serve with a green salad, if you like.

GET AHEAD
Make the pomodoro sauce up to 2 days ahead. Cool, cover and chill. Complete the recipe to serve.

Orzo Salad

Named in Italian after its resemblance to barley, orzo is a form of small rice-shaped pasta. Inspired by the flavours of a Greek salad, this recipe makes for a very satisfying meal.

FOR THE SALAD
1 vegan stock cube
250g orzo
200g fine green beans, trimmed and halved
½ medium cucumber, halved, deseeded and finely sliced
200g cherry tomatoes, quartered
½–1 red onion, finely sliced, to taste
100g pitted Kalamata olives, halved
1 red chilli, deseeded and finely chopped
Small handful mint, leaves picked and roughly chopped
Small handful parsley, roughly chopped

FOR THE DRESSING
2½ tbsp extra virgin olive oil
1 tsp dried oregano
1½ tbsp vegan red wine vinegar

Hands-on time: 20 minutes, plus cooling
Cooking time: about 10 minutes
Serves 4

PER SERVING 394cals, 11g protein, 14g fat
(2g saturates), 52g carbs (7g total sugars), 8g fibre

1. For the salad, bring a large pan of salted water to the boil and stir in the stock cube to dissolve. Add the orzo and cook according to pack instructions, adding the beans for the final 3 minutes. Drain and rinse under cold water until cool. Drain well.

2. Meanwhile, in a large shallow serving bowl, mix all the dressing ingredients with some seasoning. Add the orzo mixture and remaining salad ingredients. Mix gently and check the seasoning.

5

Slow-cooker
Suppers

Beef Stew
with Dumplings

You'll only need 20 minutes to prep this irresistible stew, and there's no need to brown the beef first.

FOR THE STEW
2 tbsp vegetable oil
1 onion, roughly chopped
2 medium parsnips, peeled and roughly chopped
2 medium carrots, peeled and roughly chopped
1 large leek, cut into roughly 1cm slices
3 tbsp tomato purée
1.2kg braising steak, cut into roughly 4cm chunks
3 tbsp plain flour
200ml red wine
600ml beef stock
3 rosemary sprigs

FOR THE DUMPLINGS
125g self-raising flour
60g suet
1 tbsp dried parsley

Hands-on time: 20 minutes
Cooking time: about 6 hours
Serves 6

PER SERVING 526cals, 38g protein, 28g fat
(12g saturates), 27g carbs (8g total sugars), 4g fibre

1. Put the oil, vegetables and tomato purée into the bowl of your slow cooker. Dry the beef pieces with kitchen paper and dust with the plain flour (tapping off excess). Add to the slow cooker together with the wine, stock, rosemary and some seasoning. Stir to combine.

2. Cover and cook on high for 5 hours or until the beef is tender.

3. After 5 hours of cooking, make the dumplings. Sift the flour into a large bowl and stir in the suet, parsley and lots of seasoning. Add 100ml cold water and mix to make a soft (and slightly sticky) dough.

4. Remove the lid of the slow cooker and discard the rosemary sprigs. Pinch off walnut-sized pieces of dough, gently roll into balls and place on top of the stew, spacing apart. Re-cover the stew and cook for 1 hour more. Check the seasoning and serve with mashed potatoes.

Lamb Tagine with Chickpeas and Olives

So easy, especially as the slow cooker does all the work. The ideal warming meal to have waiting for you after a long day.

FOR THE TAGINE
1 tbsp vegetable oil
900g lamb neck fillet, cut into rough 3cm pieces
1 large onion, finely chopped
1 tsp za'atar
1 tsp ground cinnamon
1 tsp ground cumin
1 tbsp tomato purée
400g tin chopped tomatoes
300ml chicken stock
400g tin chickpeas, drained and rinsed
100g pitted green olives
75g dried apricots, chopped

TO SERVE
Small handful mint leaves, roughly chopped
50g flaked almonds, toasted
100g natural yogurt

Hands-on time: 20 minutes
Cooking time: about 6 hours 30 minutes
Serves 6

PER SERVING 540cals, 39g protein, 34g fat
(11g saturates), 17g carbs (10g total sugars), 5g fibre

1. For the tagine, heat the oil in a large pan over medium-high heat and brown the lamb all over, in batches if needed. Using a slotted spoon, transfer the lamb to the bowl of a slow cooker.

2. Reduce the heat under the pan to medium, add the onion and a large pinch of salt and cook for 10 minutes, stirring regularly, until softened. Stir in the spices and tomato purée and cook for 1 minute, until fragrant. Transfer the mixture to the slow cooker.

3. Add the remaining tagine ingredients to the slow cooker, stir, then cover and cook on low for 6 hours, or until the lamb is cooked through and tender.

4. Check the seasoning, transfer to a warmed serving dish and garnish with the mint and almonds. Serve with a dollop of yogurt and flatbreads, couscous or rice, if you like.

FREEZE AHEAD
Prepare to end of step 3. Cool, then transfer to a freezer-safe container or food bag and freeze for up to 1 month. To serve, defrost in the fridge and reheat in a pan until piping hot. Complete the recipe.

Braised Honey Garlic Chicken and Aubergine

This Chinese restaurant-inspired dish is better than any takeaway you might be craving. If you prefer things a little spicier, add an extra spoonful of sriracha.

DF

2 tbsp vegetable oil
800g skinless chicken thigh fillets
1 large aubergine, cut into rough 3cm chunks
2cm piece fresh root ginger, peeled and grated
5 garlic cloves, crushed
100g runny honey
75ml dark soy sauce
50ml oyster sauce
1 tbsp sriracha
2 tbsp cornflour
4 spring onions, sliced
2 tsp sesame seeds
Cooked rice, to serve

Hands-on time: 20 minutes
Cooking time: about 6 hours 15 minutes
Serves 4

PER SERVING 436cals, 44g protein, 13g fat
(2g saturates), 33g carbs (25g total sugars), 3g fibre

GH TIP
No slow cooker? In step 3, return the chicken to the pan and stir in the honey, soy, oyster and sriracha sauces and 100ml water. Bring to a simmer, cover and bubble gently for 35 minutes, stirring occasionally, or until the chicken is cooked through and the aubergine is tender. Complete the recipe.

1. Heat the oil in a large, deep frying pan (that has a lid) over high heat. Brown the chicken thigh fillets all over, in batches if needed (the chicken will not be cooked through at this stage). Remove to a plate.

2. Reduce the heat to medium. Add the aubergine to the pan and quickly turn to coat in the oil. Fry for 2 minutes, then stir in the ginger and garlic and fry for 1 minute, until aromatic.

3. Transfer the chicken and aubergine mixture to a slow cooker and stir in the honey, soy, oyster and sriracha sauces. Cover and cook on low for 6 hours, until the chicken is cooked through.

4. Strain the mixture into a medium pan. Using tongs or a slotted spoon, remove the chicken to a board. In a small cup or bowl, mix the cornflour with 2 tablespoons of the pan cooking liquid to form a smooth paste. Add to the pan and bubble over medium-high heat, stirring occasionally, for 2 minutes, or until thickened.

5. Shred or slice the chicken into bite-size pieces and return to the pan with most of the spring onions to heat through. Sprinkle over the sesame seeds and the remaining spring onions, and serve with rice, if you like.

Warming Pork and Cider Casserole

It doesn't get much more comforting than a stew, and it doesn't get much easier than cooking it in a slow cooker! Fill the kitchen with welcoming aromas and enjoy a hearty meal at the end of a long day.

1kg skinless boneless pork shoulder, cut into
    bite-size pieces
50g plain flour
1 tbsp olive oil
75g pancetta, diced
500ml cider
800g potatoes, peeled and cut into large chunks
1 leek, finely sliced
150ml chicken stock
2 tbsp wholegrain mustard
100ml crème fraîche
Small handful parsley, leaves picked and
    roughly chopped

Hands-on time: 15 minutes
Cooking time: about 6 hours 20 minutes
Serves 6

PER SERVING 522cals, 44g protein, 20g fat
(9g saturates), 35g carbs (4g total sugars), 4g fibre

1. In a medium bowl, toss the pork with the flour and plenty of seasoning. Heat the oil in large frying pan over medium-high heat. Brown the pork in the frying pan, in batches if needed, removing to the bowl of a slow cooker when done. Scrape any flour paste stuck to the pan into the slow cooker.

2. Add the pancetta to the empty frying pan and fry until golden, around 3 minutes. Add the cider and bring to a simmer. Simmer for 5 minutes until reduced by two thirds. Add the pancetta and cider mixture to the bowl of the slow cooker, along with the potatoes, leek, chicken stock, mustard and some seasoning. Stir to combine.

3. Cover and cook the casserole on low for 6 hours, until the pork is tender and the potatoes are cooked through.

4. Once cooked, stir through the crème fraîche, re-cover and heat through. Stir in the parsley, check the seasoning and serve with crusty bread if you like.

Butter Halloumi Curry

We've turned the classic butter chicken curry recipe vegetarian by using halloumi. It's one of our regular recipes to make for dinner during the week and is delicious served with rice and some mango chutney or garlic naan.

8 cardamom pods
1 tsp fenugreek seeds
2 tsp cumin seeds
½ tsp cayenne pepper
1 tsp ground turmeric
2 garlic cloves, crushed
2.5cm piece fresh root ginger, peeled and grated
40g butter or ghee
1 onion, chopped
400g tin chopped tomatoes
1 tbsp tomato purée
1 tbsp mango chutney, plus extra (optional) to serve

FOR THE CURRY
500g halloumi, cut into 2cm pieces
1 cinnamon stick
100ml double cream
Large handful fresh coriander leaves, roughly chopped

Hands-on time: 15 minutes
Cooking time: about 3–5 hours
Serves 4

PER SERVING 647cals, 32g protein, 52g fat
(34g saturates), 12g carbs (11g total sugars), 2g fibre

1. With a pestle and mortar, bash open the cardamom pods and crush briefly until the seeds come out. Pick out and discard the pod husks. Add the fenugreek, cumin, cayenne and turmeric to the mortar, then crush the spices with the pestle until ground to a medium coarseness.

2. Put the ground spices in a blender with the remaining sauce ingredients, then blend until smooth. Transfer the sauce to the slow cooker and stir in the halloumi and cinnamon stick.

3. Cover with the lid and cook on low for 3–5 hours (timings may vary between slow cooker models). Remove and discard the cinnamon, stir through the cream, re-cover and heat briefly. Check the seasoning and sprinkle with coriander. Serve with rice, naan and mango chutney, if you like.

Lamb and Lentil Shepherd's Pie

This version uses lentils and lamb mince for a nutritional kick. Plus, it's topped with a sweet potato mash for a colourful alternative to the classic.

1 tsp vegetable oil
1 onion, finely chopped
2 garlic cloves, crushed
300g lamb mince (10% fat or less)
1 tbsp tomato purée
Small handful thyme, leaves picked and roughly chopped
400g tin green lentils, drained and rinsed
2 carrots, peeled and thinly sliced
500g passata
1 beef stock cube, crumbled

FOR THE MASH
600g sweet potatoes, peeled and roughly chopped
200g floury potatoes, we used Maris Piper, peeled
   and roughly chopped
25g reduced-fat butter
½–1 tsp hot smoked paprika, to taste
40g half-fat crème fraîche

Hands-on time: 25 minutes
Cooking time: about 6 hours 25 minutes
Serves 6

PER SERVING 336cals, 16g protein, 10g fat
(5g saturates), 41g carbs (13g total sugars), 9g fibre

1. Make the mash. Put all the potatoes in a large pan, cover with cold water and bring to the boil over high heat. Simmer for 15 minutes, or until very tender.

2. Drain the potatoes and leave in a colander to steam dry and cool slightly for 5 minutes. Return the potatoes to the pan and mash until smooth with a potato masher. Add the butter, paprika and crème fraîche, season well and stir together.

3. Meanwhile, heat the oil in a frying pan over medium heat. Add the onion and fry for 10 minutes, until softened. Add the garlic and fry for 1 minute, until fragrant. Add the lamb, increase the heat to high and fry until browned well all over. Stir in the tomato purée and thyme and cook for 2 minutes.

4. Scrape the lamb mixture into the bowl of a slow cooker and stir in the lentils, carrots, passata and crumbled stock cube. Spoon the mash on top. Cover and cook on low for 6 hours (see GH TIP).

GH TIP
If the bowl of your slow cooker is oven-safe (check the manual first, to be certain), transfer the shepherd's pie to a hot grill for a few minutes to brown the top before serving, if you like.

Mushroom Bourguignon

This vegan recipe is perfect for the colder months. Let your slow cooker do all the hard work and be rewarded with a rich and flavoursome stew.

25g dried porcini mushrooms
350g shallots, peeled
½ tbsp olive oil
3 garlic cloves, crushed
2 tbsp plain flour
250ml vegan vegetable stock
400ml vegan red wine
250g chestnut mushrooms, quartered
250g portobello mushrooms, thickly sliced
250g baby button mushrooms
2 large carrots, peeled and cut into 1.5cm slices
2 bay leaves
Small bunch thyme
3 parsley sprigs, plus extra to garnish
1 tsp Marmite

Hands-on time: 10 minutes
Cooking time: about 5 hours 25 minutes
Serves 4

PER SERVING 218cals, 9g protein, 3g fat (1g saturates), 16g carbs (9g total sugars), 8g fibre

1. Put the porcini mushrooms in a small bowl, pour over 150ml just-boiled water and leave to soak for 10 minutes.

2. Meanwhile, put the shallots in a heatproof bowl and cover with freshly boiled water. Leave to soak for 2–3 minutes, then drain and rinse in cold water. Trim the ends but leave the roots intact, and peel away the skins.

3. Heat the oil in a medium pan over medium heat and fry the whole shallots for 6–7 minutes, stirring occasionally, until golden, then add the garlic and cook for a further minute. Transfer the shallots to the slow cooker. Add the flour to the empty pan and cook for 1 minute. Remove the pan from the heat and slowly add the stock, beating out as many lumps of flour as possible. Gradually stir in the wine and bring to the boil for 5 minutes to reduce slightly.

4. Put the mushrooms (including the porcini in their liquid), carrots and some seasoning into the slow cooker, pour over the wine mixture and stir together.

5. Tie the bay leaves, thyme and parsley in a bundle with kitchen string and add to the slow cooker, making sure it is submerged. Cover with the lid and cook on low for 5 hours.

6. Strain the liquid into a medium pan through a fine sieve, returning the mushroom and shallot mixture to the slow cooker to keep warm and discarding the herb bundle. Add the Marmite to the pan and bring the liquid to the boil. Reduce to a simmer and simmer for 10 minutes.

7. Add the liquid back into the slow cooker, stir and check the seasoning. Sprinkle with extra chopped parsley and serve with mashed potato.

Miso Pork Ramen

This ramen couldn't be easier to make and is full of flavour. The miso will cause the ramen to look a little split, but will come together once mixed at the table.

1 litre hot chicken stock
4 tbsp dark soy sauce
1 tbsp mirin
1 tsp dark brown soft sugar
100g white miso paste
3 garlic cloves, crushed
4cm piece fresh root ginger, peeled and finely grated
600g pork shoulder steaks
200g mixed exotic mushrooms
Juice 1 lime
250g ramen or other dried noodles
2 pak choi, halved lengthways
2 spring onions, finely sliced
4 soft-boiled eggs, halved (optional; see GH TIP)

Hands-on time: 10 minutes
Cooking time: about 6 hours 10 minutes
Serves 4

PER SERVING (including eggs) 803cals, 70g protein, 3g fat (11g saturates), 51g carbs (7g total sugars), 6g fibre

1. In a large jug or bowl, whisk together the stock, soy sauce, mirin, sugar and miso paste until the sugar and miso have dissolved.

2. Put the garlic, ginger, pork and mushrooms into the bowl of the slow cooker. Pour over the stock mixture and stir well. Cover with the lid and cook on low for 6 hours, until the pork is tender and falling apart.

3. To serve, stir the lime juice into the ramen mixture in the slow cooker, breaking up any large pieces of pork, and check the seasoning. Cook the noodles according to the pack instructions, adding the pak choi for the final minute of cooking; drain.

4. Divide the noodles and pak choi among 4 deep bowls. Ladle the ramen mixture over the noodles and pak choi, making sure the pork and mushrooms are evenly distributed. Top with spring onions and add a halved egg to each bowl, if using.

GH TIP
For perfect soft-boiled eggs, bring a small pan of water to the boil, add 4 medium eggs, reduce the heat to low and simmer gently for 6 minutes. Drain, put into a large bowl of cold water to stop the cooking, and leave to cool before peeling.

GET AHEAD
Make to end of step 2, then cool, cover and chill up to 2 days ahead. Reheat on the hob until piping hot (do not boil). Complete the recipe to serve.

Lamb Ragu with Buttered Quinoa

Simple, rich and deeply satisfying. Toasting the quinoa before cooking gives it an extra nutty boost for a simple, fibre-rich side dish. If you prefer, the ragu would also be delicious served over pasta, with mash or even just hunks of bread for mopping up the sauce.

1 tbsp olive oil
400g lamb mince
1 large onion, finely chopped
2 garlic cloves, crushed
1 tbsp dried mixed herbs
2 lamb or chicken stock cubes
2 tbsp tomato purée
400g tin chopped tomatoes
450–465g jar roasted peppers, drained and thickly sliced
2 bay leaves
1 tsp sugar
225g dried quinoa
25g butter
150g baby spinach

Hands-on time: 25 minutes
Cooking time: about 4 hours 15 minutes (on high power)
Serves 4

PER SERVING 536cals, 31g protein, 26g fat
(10g saturates), 42g carbs (14g total sugars), 7g fibre

GH TIP
If you don't have a slow cooker, simply complete steps 1–3 in a large, deep frying pan (that has a lid) and simmer, covered, for 1½ hours.

1. Heat the oil in a large frying pan over high heat and lightly brown the lamb all over, stirring to break up any lumps. Remove with a slotted spoon to the bowl of a slow cooker (see GH TIP).

2. Add the onion to the pan and fry, scraping the bottom of the pan to lift up any sticky goodness, for 3–4min, or until the onion has taken on some colour. Stir in the garlic and mixed herbs, then add to the slow cooker.

3. Dissolve 1 stock cube and the tomato purée in 150ml freshly boiled water. Add to the slow cooker with the chopped tomatoes, peppers, bay leaves, sugar and plenty of seasoning. Stir, then cover with the lid and cook on high for 4 hours, or low for 8–9 hours.

4. Towards the end of cooking, prepare the quinoa. Toast the quinoa in a dry, large deep frying pan (that has a lid) over medium heat for 5 minutes, stirring occasionally. In a jug, dissolve the remaining stock cube in 450ml freshly boiled water, then stir in the butter to melt. Add the stock mixture to the quinoa and bring to the boil. Reduce the heat, cover and simmer for 12–15 minutes, or until the quinoa is tender and has absorbed the stock.

5. Uncover the slow cooker, remove and discard the bay leaves and stir in the spinach until wilted. Check the seasoning and serve with the quinoa.

6

Just 5 Ingredients

Spring Minestrone

This recipe can easily be adapted to suit different dietary requirements, or to use up leftover vegetables you may have in your fridge.

4 tbsp vegan pesto
125g small vegan pasta shapes
250g frozen vegetable mix
125g spring greens, shredded
25g vegan hard cheese alternative, grated

Hands-on time: 10 minutes
Cooking time: about 10 minutes
Serves 4

PER SERVING 466cals, 5g protein, 15g fat
(3g saturates), 76g carbs (18g total sugars), 3g fibre

1. In a large pan, bring 1.2 litres water to the boil and stir in 2 tablespoons pesto and plenty of seasoning. Add the pasta and cook according to the pack instructions, adding the frozen vegetable mix and spring greens for the final 5 minutes of cooking.

2. Check the seasoning and ladle into 4 bowls. Garnish with the remaining 2 tablespoons pesto and the cheese alternative.

Beef and Oyster Sauce Stir-fry

Oyster sauce has a complex flavour, making it an ideal base
for a simple stir-fry.

DF

2 x 255g rump steaks, excess fat removed
250g dried medium egg noodles
250g stir-fry vegetable mix
4 tbsp oyster sauce
2 tbsp salted peanuts

YOU WILL ALSO NEED
1 tbsp vegetable oil

**Hands-on time: 15 minutes, plus coming up
   to room temperature
Cooking time: about 15 minutes
Serves 4**

PER SERVING 484cals, 40g protein, 13g fat (3g
saturates), 48g carbs (3g total sugars), 6g fibre

1. Remove the steaks from the fridge and allow to
   come up to room temperature for 15 minutes.

2. Heat half a tablespoon oil in a large frying pan
   over medium-high heat. Season the steaks and
   fry for 3–3½ minutes per side for pink meat (fry
   for shorter/longer depending on the thickness
   of the meat). Set the steaks aside on a board.

3. Meanwhile, cook the noodles in a medium
   pan of boiling water according to the pack
   instructions. Drain.

4. Wipe the steak frying pan clean and return to a
   high heat with the remaining half a tablespoon
   oil. Add the vegetable mix and stir-fry for
   3 minutes, until almost tender. Slice the steaks.

5. Add the drained noodles and oyster sauce to
   the frying pan and toss to combine and heat
   through. Check the seasoning, then divide
   among 4 bowls. Top with the steaks and scatter
   over the peanuts.

Squash and Spinach Gnocchi

The starchy cooking water is the secret ingredient for turning butternut into a velvety sauce. A sprinkling of dried chilli flakes just before serving would be a delicious addition.

400g peeled and deseeded butternut squash, cut
    into rough 2cm pieces
800g gnocchi
150g spinach
200g feta, crumbled
3 tbsp mixed seeds, toasted

Hands-on time: 30 minutes
Cooking time: about 20 minutes
Serves 4

PER SERVING 545cals, 20g protein, 18g fat
(8g saturates), 70g carbs (7g total sugars), 10g fibre

1. Bring a large pan of salted water to the boil and cook the squash for 10 minutes, or until tender. Using a slotted spoon (reserve the water for cooking the gnocchi), transfer the squash to a blender.

2. Bring the cooking water back up to the boil, if needed. Add the gnocchi and cook according to the pack instructions. Drain, reserving a mugful of the starchy cooking water.

3. Add 125ml reserved cooking water to the blender, together with plenty of seasoning. Whizz until smooth.

4. Return the gnocchi to the empty pan and add the sauce and spinach. Cook over medium heat, stirring, until the spinach wilts, adding a little more of the reserved cooking water to loosen, if needed. Check seasoning.

5. Divide among 4 bowls and sprinkle over the feta and toasted mixed seeds to serve.

Honey, Mustard and Salmon Traybake

This hands-off traybake will soon become a staple weekday supper. You can leave the skin on your salmon fillets or remove it, if you prefer.

DF

850g new potatoes, halved
200g Tenderstem broccoli, roughly chopped
2 tbsp wholegrain mustard
3 tbsp runny honey
4 x salmon fillets (about 120g each)

YOU WILL ALSO NEED
2 tbsp olive oil

Hands-on time: 20 minutes
Cooking time: about 45 minutes
Serves 4

PER SERVING 541cals, 31g protein, 25g fat
(4g saturates), 45g carbs (15g total sugars), 7g fibre

1. Preheat oven to 200°C (180°C fan) mark 6. In a large bowl, toss the potatoes, broccoli, 1 tablespoon oil and plenty of seasoning. Tip just the potatoes into a medium roasting tin and cook for 30 minutes, or until beginning to turn golden, adding the broccoli for the final 10 minutes.

2. In the empty bowl, mix the mustard, honey, remaining 1 tablespoon oil and plenty of seasoning. Carefully remove the tin from the oven and mix through half the mustard mixture. Add the salmon fillets to the bowl with the remaining mustard mixture and turn to coat.

3. Arrange the fish on top of the vegetables and return the tin to the oven for 12–15 minutes, or until the salmon is cooked through and the vegetables are tender.

Easy Meatball Lasagne

Roasted peppers from a jar are the secret to the flavoursome meatball sauce in this dish. Swap the Parmesan for mature Cheddar, if you like.

400g (24) small ready-made beef meatballs
350g jarred peppers (drained weight)
75g Parmesan, grated
150g fresh lasagne sheets
350g fresh cheese sauce

YOU WILL ALSO NEED
2 tsp olive oil

Hands-on time: 15 minutes
Cooking time: about 40 minutes
Serves 4

PER SERVING 570cals, 34g protein, 35g fat
(17g saturates), 30g carbs (2g total sugars), 2g fibre

1. Preheat oven to 200°C (180°C fan) mark 6. Heat the oil in a large frying pan over medium heat. Add the meatballs and fry, turning regularly, for 5–6 minutes, until browned all over. Remove and safely discard all but 3 tablespoons of the oil.

2. Meanwhile, thickly slice the peppers. Whizz 200g in the small bowl of a food processor, or with a stick blender, until smooth. Add the pepper purée and some seasoning to the browned meatballs and cook for 1 minute, stirring to scrape up any caramelised bits from the pan.

3. Spoon half the meatball mixture into a 1.8–2 litre ovenproof dish and spread it out evenly. Sprinkle over half the remaining sliced peppers and a handful of Parmesan. Arrange half the lasagne sheets on top and spread over half the cheese sauce. Repeat layers once more, finishing with a scattering of Parmesan and some freshly ground black pepper.

4. Cover the ovenproof dish with foil and cook for 30–35 minutes, removing the foil for the final 15 minutes, or until browned and bubbling.

GH TIP
If you love cheese, add some sliced mozzarella along with the Parmesan.

Chicken and Mushroom Pie

Comforting for chilly days and so speedy to pull together, this is sure to become a regular midweek favourite.

350g chicken thigh fillets, cut into rough 2cm pieces
200g chestnut mushrooms, halved and sliced
295g tin condensed cream of mushroom soup (see GH TIP)
100g frozen peas
320g sheet puff pastry

YOU WILL ALSO NEED
1 tbsp vegetable or olive oil

Hands-on time: 15 minutes
Cooking time: about 45 minutes
Serves 4

PER SERVING 425cals, 26g protein, 23g fat (9g saturates), 27g carbs (2g total sugars), 3g fibre

1. Heat the oil in a large pan over medium-high heat. Add the chicken and brown all over. Remove to a bowl. Add the mushrooms and fry for 5 minutes, or until tender and any liquid in the pan has evaporated.

2. Preheat oven to 200°C (180°C fan) mark 6. Add the mushrooms to the chicken bowl and mix in the mushroom soup, peas and some seasoning. Empty into a rough 1.7 litre ovenproof frying pan or serving dish.

3. Cover with the pastry and crimp the edges to the dish to seal. Trim excess pastry, then cut a steam hole into the centre of the pie. Cook in the oven for 30 minutes, or until golden and bubbling. Serve with a green salad, if you like.

GH TIP
Using condensed soup boosts the flavour of the filling. You can use a 400g tin of regular mushroom soup instead, but the pie sauce will be loose.

Tapenade Lamb Chops with Bulgur Wheat

Green olive tapenade gives a delicate, vaguely Mediterranean flavour. If you don't want to use feta, some finely grated lemon zest and juice sprinkled over the dish at the end would be delicious.

2 large courgettes, thickly sliced
8 lamb loin chops
5 tbsp green olive tapenade
200g bulgur wheat
75g feta, crumbled

YOU WILL ALSO NEED
2 tsp olive oil

Hands-on time: 15 minutes
Cooking time: about 12 minutes
Serves 4

PER SERVING 816cals, 42g protein, 53g fat (23g saturates), 40g carbs (3g total sugars), 5g fibre

1. Preheat grill to high. Toss the courgettes with the oil and some seasoning and spread out on a large non-stick baking tray. Brush the lamb chops with 2 tablespoons tapenade. Arrange the chops on top of the courgettes and season with plenty of freshly ground black pepper.

2. Grill for 10–12 minutes, turning the chops and courgettes halfway through, or until the meat is golden-brown and the courgettes are tender.

3. Meanwhile, cook the bulgur wheat in a medium pan of salted boiling water for 8–10 minutes, until just tender. Carefully remove a small cupful of the starchy cooking water, then drain thoroughly.

4. In a small bowl, whisk the remaining 3 tablespoons tapenade with just enough of the cooking water to give a drizzling consistency. Divide the bulgur wheat, courgettes and lamb chops among 4 plates, top with the feta and a drizzle of tapenade.

Chicken on
Cheesy Leeks

If you prefer, stuff the chicken breasts with the leek
mixture (no need to add water) before wrapping them
in the Parma ham.

3 leeks, finely sliced
150g pack Boursin
4 skinless chicken breasts
8 Parma ham slices
75g ciabatta-style bread, torn into small pieces

YOU WILL ALSO NEED
3 tbsp olive oil

Hands-on time: 15 minutes
Cooking time: about 40 minutes
Serves 4

PER SERVING 445cals, 41g protein, 25g fat
(13g saturates), 12g carbs (3g total sugars), 4g fibre

1. Preheat oven to 190°C (170°C fan) mark 5. Heat
   1 tablespoon oil in a large pan and gently fry the
   leeks for 15 minutes until completely softened.
   Stir in the Boursin and 100ml water. Check
   the seasoning, then tip into an about 1.5 litre
   ovenproof serving dish.

2. Wrap each chicken breast in 2 Parma ham slices
   and nestle into the leeks. Toss the ciabatta with
   2 tablespoons olive oil and some seasoning.
   Scatter over the top. Cook for 20-25 minutes,
   until the chicken is cooked through and topping
   is golden. Serve with seasonal greens, if you like.

Lamb Mince Curry

Using minced lamb makes this quick to make. Choose any
curry paste you like (increase the quantity if you want
it spicy) and serve with rice or naan bread.

500g lamb mince
500g butternut squash (prepared weight), peeled,
   deseeded and cut into 1.5cm dice
2 tbsp curry paste, we used tikka masala
400ml tin coconut milk
150g spinach

YOU WILL ALSO NEED
1 tbsp olive oil

Hands-on time: 15 minutes
Cooking time: about 35 minutes
Serves 4

PER SERVING 553cals, 29g protein, 39g fat
(23g saturates), 19g carbs (8g total sugars), 4g fibre

1. Heat the olive oil in a large deep frying pan over
   a medium-high heat. Fry the lamb (in batches)
   until well browned. Use a slotted spoon to lift
   into a bowl and discard excess fat, if needed.
   Return the pan to a medium heat and add the
   squash. Fry for about 8–10 minutes until
   beginning to caramelise.

2. Return the lamb to the pan with the curry
   paste and fry for 1 minute, stirring. Add 300ml
   just-boiled water, then bring to a simmer and
   bubble for 15 minutes until the squash is tender.

3. Add the coconut milk and bubble for a few
   minutes. Fold through the spinach to wilt and
   season well to taste.

7

Easy Chicken Dinners

Warm Miso Chicken and Broccoli Salad with Kefir Dressing

This hearty salad is full of gut-friendly ingredients. Miso, kefir and raw cider vinegar all contain probiotics (friendly bacteria), while apples, oranges, broccoli and almonds are all good sources of soluble fibre. Plus, they taste delicious together, too!

FOR THE SALAD
3 skinless chicken breasts
2 tbsp brown miso paste
2 tsp maple syrup
2 tsp vegetable oil
200g Tenderstem broccoli
2 x 250g pouches mixed grains
2 small oranges, separated into segments
1 red-skinned apple, cored, cut into matchsticks
1 tbsp (raw) cider vinegar
25g skin-on almonds, roughly chopped

FOR THE DRESSING
125ml kefir (see GH TIP)
1 small garlic clove, crushed
1 tsp fish sauce
1 tsp (raw) cider vinegar
Small handful mint leaves, finely chopped

Hands-on time: 15 minutes
Cooking time: about 25 minutes
Serves 4

PER SERVING 536cals, 43g protein, 18g fat
(3g saturates), 46g carbs (16g total sugars), 9g fibre

GH TIP
Unflavoured kefir – either in a pot or in a bottle for drinking – will work for this recipe.

1. Preheat oven to 200°C (180°C fan) mark 6. For the salad, slash the chicken breasts several times with a knife. In a small bowl, mix the miso paste, maple syrup and 1 teaspoon oil, then rub this mixture all over the chicken.

2. Put the broccoli in a single layer in a medium roasting tin and toss through the remaining 1 teaspoon oil. Lay the chicken on top and add 2 tablespoons water to the tin, cover with foil and roast for 20–25 minutes, or until the chicken is cooked through.

3. Meanwhile, in a small bowl, mix all the dressing ingredients with plenty of freshly ground black pepper and set aside.

4. When the chicken is nearly done, heat the grains according to the pack instructions. Tip into a large bowl. Transfer the chicken to a board and add the broccoli and any juices from the tin to the grains, along with the fruit, vinegar and some seasoning. Toss gently to combine.

5. Thickly slice the chicken. Arrange the salad on a large serving platter and top with the chicken. Scatter over the almonds and drizzle over the kefir dressing to serve.

Chicken Pozole

This Mexican stew is traditionally made with hominy — corn kernels that have been soaked in a mineral lime solution — but we've used chickpeas instead. The toppings bring this dish to life.

1 tbsp vegetable oil
325g chicken thigh fillets, cut into bite-size pieces
2 garlic cloves, crushed
2 tsp ground cumin
1½ tbsp freshly chopped oregano (or use 1 tsp dried)
1-2 green chillies, to taste, deseeded and finely chopped
1 litre strong chicken stock
2 plum tomatoes, chopped
2 x 400g tins chickpeas, drained and rinsed

TO SERVE
½ iceberg lettuce, shredded
Lime wedges
6 radishes, finely sliced
½ red onion, finely sliced
1 avocado, destoned and sliced
Large handful coriander, roughly chopped

Hands-on time: 20 minutes
Cooking time: about 10 minutes
Serves 4

PER SERVING 439cals, 31g protein, 22g fat
(5g saturates), 24g carbs (4g total sugars), 11g fibre

1. Heat the oil in a large, deep frying pan over medium–high heat. Add the chicken and fry until lightly golden (it doesn't need to be cooked through yet). Stir in the garlic, cumin, oregano and chillies and fry for 1 minute, until aromatic.

2. Pour in the stock and bring to the boil. Add the tomatoes and chickpeas and simmer for a couple of minutes until tomatoes begin to break down. Check the seasoning, then ladle into 4 bowls and bring to the table with the garnishes to let people add their favourites.

Sticky Chicken Livers and Grapes on Toast

If you've never tried chicken livers, this incredibly nutritious and delicious recipe, with its sweet and tangy sauce, is a great place to start.

½ small red onion, finely sliced
Juice 1 lemon
300g free-range chicken livers
2 tsp olive oil
50g butter, in small pieces
100g seedless grapes, we used a mix of green and red
2 tbsp balsamic glaze
Small handful parsley, roughly chopped
4 small slices sourdough bread, toasted

Hands-on time: 20 minutes
Cooking time: about 10 minutes
Serves 2

PER SERVING 555cals, 32g protein, 28g fat
(15g saturates), 43g carbs (15g total sugars), 4g fibre

1. In a small non-metallic bowl, mix the onion, lemon juice and a big pinch of salt. Set aside.

2. Dry the chicken livers with kitchen paper and trim off any sinews or green/dark patches (this is easiest with scissors).

3. Heat the oil in a large frying pan over high heat. Add the livers and cook for 4 minutes, turning once, until well browned. Stir in the butter, grapes, balsamic glaze and some seasoning. Cook for 2 minutes. Remove from the heat and add most of the parsley.

4. Top the toasted sourdough with the livers and grapes, spooning over the buttery sauce. Drain the onion, scatter over the livers and sprinkle over the remaining parsley.

Spicy Chicken Peanut Noodles

On the table in minutes and packed with flavour, this will be a recipe you turn to time and time again.

1 tbsp vegetable oil
300g chicken thigh fillets, cut into finger-size strips
200g egg noodles
125g green beans, trimmed and cut into shorter lengths
3cm piece fresh root ginger, peeled and finely grated
1 red chilli, finely sliced
3 spring onions, finely sliced
25g roasted salted peanuts

FOR THE PEANUT SAUCE
75g peanut butter, crunchy or smooth
2 tbsp soy sauce
1 tbsp rice vinegar
1 tbsp sriracha

Hands-on time: 15 minutes
Cooking time: about 15 minutes
Serves 4

PER SERVING 464cals, 30g protein, 19g fat
(4g saturates), 30g carbs (4g total sugars), 6g fibre

1. Bring a large pan of water to the boil. Meanwhile, heat the oil in a large, deep frying pan or wok over medium–high heat. Fry the chicken for 5 minutes, until golden and cooked through.

2. Cook the noodles and beans in the boiling water for 5 minutes, or until tender. Drain. In a jug, whisk all the sauce ingredients together with 125ml just-boiled water, until combined.

3. Add the ginger to the chicken pan and fry for 1 minute. Add the sauce and heat through until melted and combined. Add the drained noodles and beans and toss to coat and heat through.

4. Garnish with chilli, spring onions and peanuts, and serve immediately.

Smoky Paprika Chicken Traybake

This may not be the quickest midweek recipe, but it is one of the easiest – the oven does all of the work for you, so you can get on with other things.

4 skin-on, bone-in chicken thighs
300g miniature new potatoes
1 large red pepper, deseeded and cut into large chunks
1 tbsp olive oil
3 garlic cloves, crushed
2 tsp smoked paprika (sweet or hot)
150g cherry tomatoes
1 lemon, cut into 6 wedges
4 thyme sprigs

Hands-on time: 10 minutes
Cooking time: about 1 hour
Serves 2

PER SERVING 767cals, 49g protein, 50g fat
(13g saturates), 29g carbs (7g total sugars), 5g fibre

1. Preheat oven to 200°C (180°C fan) mark 6. In a medium roasting tin, mix the chicken thighs, potatoes, pepper, oil, garlic, paprika and some seasoning. Spread into a single layer (with chicken skin-side up). Roast for 30 minutes.

2. Add the tomatoes, lemon wedges and thyme to the tin and stir gently. Return to the oven for a further 25–30 minutes, until the chicken is cooked through and the potatoes are golden and tender.

Chicken Burgers

Use leftover lean chicken from a Sunday roast to make these gastro-style burgers.

25g butter
1 shallot, finely chopped
2 rashers smoked streaky bacon, finely chopped
400g mushrooms, finely chopped
50ml white wine
1 thyme sprig, leaves removed
200g cooked chicken, finely chopped
50g fresh white breadcrumbs
1 large egg, beaten
Large handful curly parsley, roughly chopped
½ tbsp wholegrain mustard
1 tbsp olive oil
4 burger buns, split in half and toasted
A few lettuce leaves and pickle, to serve (optional)

Hands-on time: 15 minutes, plus chilling
Cooking time: about 15 minutes
Makes 4 burgers

PER BURGER (without lettuce and pickle) 373cals, 26g protein, 18g fat (10g saturates), 15g carbs (1g total sugars), 1g fibre

1. Melt the butter in a pan and gently fry the shallot and bacon for 2–3 minutes. Turn up the heat and add the mushrooms. Cook for 3–5 minutes, until tender. Add the wine and thyme and bubble until any liquid has evaporated. Set aside and allow to cool.

2. Put the chicken into a bowl with the mushroom mixture, breadcrumbs, egg, parsley and mustard. Mix well. Form into 4 burgers, squeezing each one together well to help it stick. Chill the patties for 30 minutes to firm up.

3. Heat the oil in a large frying pan and sizzle the burgers for 5 minutes, turning once. Serve in the buns, topped with lettuce leaves and a little pickle, if you like.

Lemongrass Chicken with Rice

This Vietnamese-inspired dish is an easy yet impressive meal – perfect for when friends come round midweek.

200g jasmine rice, rinsed under cold water
400ml chicken stock
2 lemongrass sticks, trimmed and finely chopped
1 red chilli, deseeded and finely chopped
5cm piece fresh root ginger, peeled and finely grated
2 tbsp sweet chilli sauce, plus extra to drizzle
4 tbsp soy sauce
2 tbsp cornflour
2 tbsp fish sauce
4 skinless chicken breasts, cut into finger-size strips
8 spring onions, finely sliced
2 tbsp vegetable oil

Hands-on time: 20 minutes
Cooking time: about 15 minutes
Serves 4

PER SERVING 472cals, 44g protein, 8g fat
(1g saturates), 57g carbs (10g total sugars), 1g fibre

1. Mix the rice and stock in a medium pan (that has a lid). Cover and bring to the boil over high heat. Reduce the heat to low and cook for 5 minutes, then remove the pan from the heat and leave to steam (with the lid on) for 10 minutes. Remove the lid and fluff up the rice with a fork.

2. Meanwhile, in a large bowl mix the lemongrass, chilli, ginger, sweet chilli and soy sauces, cornflour, fish sauce, chicken and most of the spring onions.

3. Heat the oil in a large non-stick frying pan or wok over high heat. Add the chicken mixture and stir-fry for 8–10 minutes, or until the chicken is cooked through. Garnish with the remaining spring onions and a drizzle of sweet chilli sauce. Serve with the rice.

Teriyaki Chicken with Noodle Salad

Lively flavours such as ginger, chilli and garlic mean you don't need to use as much oil in this recipe.

4 skinless chicken breasts
3 tbsp teriyaki sauce
1 tbsp clear honey
2.5cm fresh root ginger, peeled and grated
2 garlic cloves, crushed
1 tbsp olive oil

FOR THE NOODLE SALAD
400g ready-cooked rice noodles
150g sugar snap peas
100g fresh or frozen soya (edamame) or broad beans,
    podded and shelled
4 tbsp sweet chilli sauce
1 tbsp dark soy sauce
1 green chilli, deseeded and finely chopped
Finely grated zest and juice 1 lime
1 tbsp each freshly chopped coriander and mint

Hands-on time: 15 minutes, plus marinating
Cooking time: about 15 minutes
Serves 4

PER SERVING 459cals, 36g protein, 10g fat
(2g saturates), 55g carbs (20g total sugars), 3g fibre

1. Put the chicken on a board, cover with clingfilm and flatten with a rolling pin until it's an even thickness of about 1cm. Mix together the teriyaki sauce, honey, ginger, garlic and oil in a large non-metallic bowl. Add the chicken and coat thoroughly. Cover and marinate for 30 minutes or overnight in the fridge.

2. Preheat grill to medium and set the rack about 15cm away from the heat. Put the chicken on a foil-lined baking sheet; grill for 6–7 minutes on each side until cooked through, brushing frequently with any leftover marinade.

3. Reheat the noodles according to the pack instructions. Drain. Cook the sugar snap peas and soya or broad beans for 2–3 minutes in salted, boiling water until just tender. Drain and add to the noodles.

4. Mix together the remaining ingredients and toss with the noodles. Divide among 4 plates. Thickly slice the chicken, then put on top of the noodles. Serve hot or at room temperature.

Chicken Cacciatore

This low-calorie chicken dish is easy to make and takes 30 minutes to cook.

DF

1 tbsp olive oil
4 skinless chicken breasts
1 onion, chopped
250g white mushrooms, sliced
2 x 400g tins chopped tomatoes
1 tsp dried oregano
1 bay leaf
150ml chicken stock
Large handful rocket

Hands-on time: 10 minutes
Cooking time: about 30 minutes
Serves 4

PER SERVING 252cals, 39g protein, 5g fat
(1g saturates), 11g carbs (10g total sugars), 3g fibre

1. Heat half the oil in a large, deep frying pan. Fry the chicken over a high heat for 6 minutes, turning once. Lift the chicken out and set aside on a plate.

2. Heat the remaining oil in the pan and fry the onion and mushrooms over a medium heat for 8 minutes, until beginning to soften. Stir in the tomatoes, oregano, bay leaf and chicken stock. Return the chicken to the pan, bring the mixture to the boil, then simmer for 15 minutes, turning the chicken midway, or until cooked through and the sauce has thickened.

3. Remove the bay leaf, then season well and stir through the rocket. Serve with seasonal vegetables or crusty bread to mop up the juices.

One-pot Lemon Chicken and Orzo

This dish couldn't be simpler, yet still packs a flavour punch.
Buy the best-quality chicken you can afford for the optimum
taste and texture.

DF

1 tbsp olive oil
8 skin-on chicken thighs (about 800g–1kg)
2 leeks, finely sliced
300g orzo pasta
700ml hot chicken stock
Finely grated zest and juice 1 lemon

Hands-on time: 20 minutes
Cooking time: about 50 minutes
Serves 4

PER SERVING 622cals, 58g protein, 16g fat
(4g saturates), 58g carbs (4g total sugars), 7g fibre

1. Heat the oil in a large, shallow casserole dish
   (that has a lid) over medium heat. Add the
   chicken thighs and brown all over, in batches
   if needed. Remove to a bowl.

2. Add the leeks to the casserole dish and cook
   for 8–10 minutes, scraping up any sticky brown
   goodness from the base of the dish, or until
   softened. Stir in the orzo, stock, lemon zest,
   juice and plenty of seasoning.

3. Bring to the boil, stirring to make sure the orzo
   isn't sticking to the base of the dish. Lay the
   chicken on top of the orzo (skin-side up). Cover
   and simmer for 20–25 minutes, or until the orzo
   is tender and the chicken is cooked through.
   Serve with a salad or seasonal greens, if you like.

8

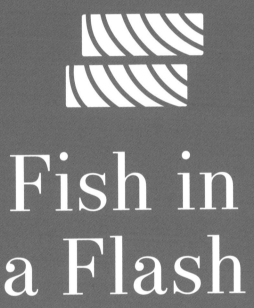

Fish in
a Flash

Simple Seafood Chowder

If you can't get hold of fish pie mix, use the same weight of your favourite skinless fish fillets, chopped into rough 2cm chunks.

1 tbsp olive oil
3 smoked streaky bacon rashers, roughly chopped
2 spring onions, finely sliced
400g new potatoes, cut into rough 1cm chunks
350g fish pie mix, defrosted if frozen (see intro)
600ml fish stock
198g tin sweetcorn, drained
125ml double cream
Small handful parsley, roughly chopped

Hands-on time: 20 minutes
Cooking time: about 20 minutes
Serves 4

PER SERVING 440cals, 25g protein, 27g fat (13g saturates), 22g carbs (5g total sugars), 3g fibre

1. Heat the oil in a large non-stick pan over medium heat and cook the bacon, spring onions and potatoes for 5 minutes, or until the onions have softened and the bacon and potatoes are starting to crisp.

2. Stir in the fish pie mix, stock and some seasoning. Bring to the boil and simmer for 10–12 minutes, or until the fish is cooked through and the liquid is slightly thickened.

3. Stir in the sweetcorn and cream and heat through. Check the seasoning. Sprinkle over the parsley and divide among 4 bowls. Serve with crusty bread, if you like.

Mussels with Cider and Samphire

As well as being delicious, mussels are relatively affordable and nutritious. Samphire is now more widely available in supermarkets, but you can also forage it yourself in estuaries, mudflats and salt marshes all around the UK.

2kg fresh mussels
50g butter
8 spring onions, finely sliced
Large handful parsley, stalks and leaves separated and finely chopped
500ml cider (check it's gluten free)
250g samphire
200ml double cream

Hands-on time: 35 minutes, including cleaning the mussels
Cooking time: about 15 minutes
Serves 4

PER SERVING 538cals, 27g protein, 40g fat (24g saturates), 7g carbs (6g total sugars), 4g fibre

1. Put the mussels into a colander and rinse under cold running water. Scrape off any barnacles using a cutlery knife and pull off and discard any stringy beards. Throw away any mussels that don't close when tapped firmly (it's okay if they open again).

2. Melt the butter in a large, deep pan (that has a lid) over low-medium heat. Add the spring onions, parsley stalks and some seasoning and cook for 3 minutes, until slightly softened.

3. Increase the heat to high, add the cider and bring to a simmer. Stir through the mussels, cover with the lid and cook for 8–10 minutes, shaking the pan occasionally and adding the samphire for the final 5 minutes. The cooked mussels should be fully open (discard any that remain closed).

4. Mix through the cream and chopped parsley leaves. Serve immediately with some crusty bread, if you like, for mopping up the sauce.

Salmon and Noodle Parcels

Mix up the veggies in these parcels to suit your preference. Not a fan of pak choi? Thinly sliced pepper or a handful of spinach works, too.

DF

Juice 2 limes, plus extra wedges to serve
3 tbsp soy sauce
550g cooked/fresh egg noodles
2 pak choi, quartered lengthways
4 salmon fillets, skin removed if you prefer
5cm piece fresh root ginger, peeled and thinly sliced into matchsticks
1 red chilli, deseeded and thinly sliced
Small handful coriander, roughly torn

Hands-on time: 10 minutes
Cooking time: about 20 minutes
Serves 4

PER SERVING 523cals, 34g protein, 22g fat
(4g saturates), 46g carbs (3g total sugars), 4g fibre

1. Preheat oven to 200°C (180°C fan) mark 6. Arrange 4 rough 40cm squares of baking parchment on a work surface. In a small bowl, mix the lime juice, soy sauce and plenty of seasoning. Arrange the noodles in mounds in the centre of the squares and toss through half the soy sauce mixture. Top each noodle mound with 2 quarters of pak choi, then lay on the salmon fillets.

2. Mix the ginger and chilli into the remaining soy mixture, then spoon over the salmon fillets.

3. Working 1 at a time, lift the sides of the baking parchment up and over the filling and roll down the edges to seal (leaving some space above the fish). Transfer the parcels to a large baking tray and cook for 18-20 minutes, or until the fish feels firm when pressed.

4. Carefully open the parcels and sprinkle over the coriander. Transfer to 4 plates (either in the parcels or removed from them) and serve with the lime wedges.

Mackerel and Roasted Broccoli Noodle Salad

For a change from wheat-based dishes, look out for soba noodles that are 100% buckwheat. Any leftovers are delicious served straight from the fridge.

1 tbsp olive oil
200g Tenderstem broccoli, chopped
250g pak choi, stalks thickly shredded, leaves left whole
275g buckwheat soba noodles
1 tbsp toasted sesame oil
2 nori seaweed sheets
125g smooth peanut butter
1 red chilli, deseeded and finely chopped
½ tbsp sugar
250g hot smoked mackerel

Hands-on time: 20 minutes
Cooking time: about 20 minutes
Serves 4

PER SERVING 739cals, 37g protein, 39g fat
(8g saturates), 52g carbs (7g total sugars), 11g fibre

1. Preheat oven to 180°C (160°C fan) mark 4. In a large roasting tin, toss the oil, broccoli, pak choi and plenty of seasoning. Roast for 20 minutes, stirring halfway, until tender.

2. Meanwhile, cook the soba noodles in a medium pan of salted water according to the pack instructions. Drain, then briefly rinse under cold water; drain again. Empty into a large bowl and toss through the sesame oil.

3. Using kitchen scissors or a sharp knife, quarter the nori seaweed sheets, then snip/slice into thin strips. In a small pan, gently heat the peanut butter, chilli, sugar, 3 tablespoons water and some seasoning, whisking until combined and hot.

4. Add the peanut butter mixture to the noodles along with the vegetables, and mix. Skin the mackerel (if you like), then flake it into the noodle mixture and add half the shredded nori. Carefully mix, then divide among 4 bowls and sprinkle over the remaining nori to serve.

Prawn Cocktail Burger

All the flavours of prawn cocktail in a tasty burger!
The patties will be soft, so grease liberally to prevent
them from sticking to the bars of your grill.

450g raw peeled king prawns
4 spring onions, roughly chopped
1 tbsp sundried tomato paste
250g pork mince
2 tbsp cornflour
Vegetable oil, to grease and rub

TO SERVE
6 brioche or sesame burger buns, split
1 ripe avocado, halved, stoned and thinly sliced
Juice ½ lemon
6 tbsp seafood/Marie Rose sauce
6 large pickled gherkin slices
¼ iceberg lettuce, shredded

Hands-on time: 25 minutes, plus chilling
Cooking time: about 20 minutes
Makes 6 burgers

PER BURGER 524cals, 29g protein, 28g fat
(8g saturates), 37g carbs (5g total sugars), 3g fibre

GET AHEAD
Prepare to the end of step
1 up to a day ahead. Keep
chilled. Complete the recipe
to serve.

1. For the burgers, pulse 300g of the prawns in a
   food processor with the spring onions, sundried
   tomato paste, 1½ teaspoons fine salt and some
   freshly ground black pepper until finely
   chopped. Empty into a large bowl. Roughly chop
   the remaining 150g prawns and add to the bowl
   with the pork mince and cornflour. Mix
   thoroughly (using your hands is easiest) and
   form into 6 patties. Arrange on a lightly greased
   plate, then cover and chill for 2 hours, to firm up.

2. Rub the patties with oil, then barbecue or griddle
   over low heat for 15–18 minutes, turning halfway,
   or until cooked through. Towards the end of
   cooking, barbecue or griddle the burger buns
   (cut-side down), until toasted.

3. To serve, in a small bowl toss the avocado
   slices and lemon juice. Spread half a tablespoon
   seafood/Marie Rose sauce over the bases of the
   toasted buns. Drain the avocado and lay on
   to the bases, then top with the burger patties,
   gherkin slices and some shredded lettuce.
   Add a drizzle more seafood/Marie Rose sauce
   to each and finish with the burger lids.

Chilli and Ginger Salmon Kebabs

The processor does most of the work needed for these fragrant fish kebabs. Drop the chilli for a milder flavour.

2 garlic cloves
1 lemongrass stick, roughly chopped
5cm piece fresh root ginger, peeled and roughly chopped
2 spring onions, roughly chopped
2 red chillies, deseeded and roughly chopped
Small handful coriander
4 salmon fillets (roughly 125g each)
1 tbsp soy sauce
150g fresh white breadcrumbs
1 medium egg white
1 tbsp vegetable oil

FOR THE DIPPING SAUCE
175g Greek-style yogurt
1½ tbsp sweet chilli sauce

YOU WILL ALSO NEED
6 wooden skewers, soaked in water for 30 minutes

Hands-on time: 30 minutes, plus chilling
Cooking time: about 15 minutes
Makes 6 kebabs

PER KEBAB 330cals, 23g protein, 16g fat
(4g saturates), 23g carbs (5g total sugars), 0g fibre

1. In a food processor, pulse the garlic, lemongrass, ginger, spring onions, chillies and coriander (leaves and stalks) until finely chopped. Skin the salmon (if needed) and add to the processor with the soy sauce, breadcrumbs, egg white and plenty of seasoning.

2. Pulse until fairly smooth and combined. Empty into a bowl and, with damp hands, divide into 6. Shape each portion either into 5 balls or sausage shapes and skewer. Place on a non-stick baking tray and chill for 30 minutes.

3. Brush the oil all over the kebabs and barbecue or griddle over medium heat for 15 minutes, carefully turning halfway, until golden and cooked through.

4. Meanwhile, in a serving bowl, mix the yogurt with plenty of seasoning, then ripple through the sweet chilli sauce. Serve with the kebabs.

GET AHEAD
Prepare to end of step
2 up to 4 hours ahead.
Keep chilled. Complete
the recipe to serve.

Curried Fish Dhal Traybake

Swap the cod for haddock or salmon fillets, and the curry paste for a spicier variety, if you prefer.

2 tbsp olive oil
3½ tbsp medium curry paste (check it's gluten free)
175g natural yogurt
4 skinless cod fillets (about 125g each)
25g coriander, stalks and leaves
250g red split lentils, well rinsed

Hands-on time: 20 minutes
Cooking time: about 55 minutes
Serves 4

PER SERVING 412cals, 39g protein, 11g fat
(3g saturates), 38g carbs (6g total sugars), 4g fibre

1. Preheat oven to 200°C (180°C fan) mark 6. Pour the oil into a medium roasting tin and put into the oven to heat for 10 minutes.

2. In a large bowl, mix 1 tablespoon curry paste with 100g yogurt and plenty of seasoning. Add the fish and turn gently to coat. Cover and chill until needed.

3. Reserve a few coriander leaves for garnish and roughly chop the remaining leaves and stalks. Carefully remove the roasting tin from the oven and gently stir in the lentils, 2 tablespoons curry paste, the chopped coriander and plenty of seasoning. Pour in 700ml just-boiled water from a kettle and return to the oven for 25–30 minutes, or until the lentils are nearly tender and have absorbed most of the liquid.

4. Carefully remove the roasting tin from the oven and add the fish fillets. Return to the oven for 12–15 minutes, or until the fish is cooked through.

5. In a bowl, mix the remaining 75g yogurt with plenty of seasoning. Swirl though the remaining half a tablespoon curry paste. Spoon the yogurt mixture on to the fish and lentils (or serve alongside) and scatter over the remaining coriander leaves.

Prosciutto Wrapped Trout

You can use other firm fish fillets in this recipe, but the flavours of sea trout and Jersey Royal potatoes when they're in season are hard to beat.

750g new potatoes
1 small shallot, finely chopped
150ml dry white wine
Juice ½ lemon
100g unsalted butter
1 tbsp capers, roughly chopped
Small bunch of parsley, roughly chopped
4 trout fillets, skinned and deboned
8 slices prosciutto ham
Oil, to grease
250g cherry tomatoes on the vine
4 spring onions, sliced
40g Parmesan, grated

Hands-on time: 15 minutes
Cooking time: about 35 minutes
Serves 4

PER SERVING 677cals, 43g protein, 39g fat
(20g saturates), 32g carbs (5g total sugars), 4g fibre

1. In a large pan of boiling water, simmer the new potatoes for 15–20 minutes until cooked through. Drain and crush with a fork. Set aside.

2. Make the sauce: into a small pan over a medium heat, put the shallot, wine and lemon juice, and bubble until reduced by two-thirds (5–8 minutes). Cube 75g of the butter and add to the pan, whisking to combine. Stir in the capers and parsley. Set aside and keep warm.

3. Preheat grill to medium-high. Wrap each trout fillet with 2 slices of prosciutto. Put on to a lightly oiled baking tray with the cherry tomatoes. Season with salt and pepper. Grill the fillets for 4 minutes each side, until the ham is crisp, and the fish and tomatoes are cooked.

4. Meanwhile, add the remaining butter to a large frying pan and gently fry the spring onions for 2 minutes. Add the crushed potatoes and Parmesan, and heat for a few minutes before seasoning with salt and pepper. Serve the fish with the crushed new potatoes, cherry tomatoes and parsley butter sauce.

Sunshine
Fish Pie

With a ready-made soup to create the sauce and a pre-made
mash topping, this has to be the easiest fish pie ever!

600g tub fresh tomato soup
800g mixed fish and seafood (we used cod
    and raw prawns)
2 x 400g packs ready-made mashed potato
1 tbsp Dijon mustard
75g grated mature Cheddar
Small bunch finely chopped parsley

Hands-on time: 10 minutes
Cooking time: about 50 minutes
Serves 4

PER SERVING 507cals, 46g protein, 21g fat
(11g saturates), 31g carbs (8g total sugars), 6g fibre

1. Preheat oven to 200°C (180°C fan) mark 6.
   In a medium pan, bring the tomato soup to the
   boil and bubble to reduce it to a thick sauce
   consistency – about 15 minutes (the fish juices
   will thin it down).

2. Meanwhile, chop the mixed fish and seafood into
   large chunks, if needed. Mix into the soup, then
   tip into a 1.4 litre pie dish.

3. In a large bowl, mix together the mashed potato,
   mustard, Cheddar and chopped parsley. Spoon
   over the fish mixture. Bake for 30–35 minutes
   until golden and bubbling.

Crispy Salmon Teriyaki Stir-fry

Brushing the salmon with cornflour helps to crisp it up and creates great texture. Ready in just 25 minutes, this noodle dish is nutritious and better than a takeaway any day.

DF

4 skin-on salmon fillets
1 tbsp cornflour
½ tbsp vegetable oil
½ tbsp sesame oil
300g stir-fry vegetable mix
300g fresh egg noodles

FOR THE SAUCE
6 tbsp teriyaki sauce
Juice ½ lime
2 garlic cloves, crushed
3cm piece fresh root ginger, peeled and finely grated
½ red chilli, deseeded and finely chopped

Hands-on time: 15 minutes
Cooking time: about 10 minutes
Serves 4

PER SERVING 548cals, 35g protein, 28g fat
(5g saturates), 36g carbs (13g total sugars), 3g fibre

1. In a small bowl, mix together the sauce ingredients. Using a pastry brush, brush the salmon lightly on all sides with the cornflour. Heat the vegetable oil in a large non-stick frying pan over medium heat.

2. Fry the salmon fillets skin-side down for 5 minutes, then flip and fry for 2 minutes more. Add half the sauce and cook until sticky, spooning the sauce over the salmon to coat.

3. Meanwhile, in a separate medium frying pan or wok, heat the sesame oil over high heat. Add the vegetable stir-fry pack and stir-fry for 3 minutes, until just tender. Add the remaining sauce and the noodles and cook until piping hot and coated in the sauce.

4. Divide the noodle mixture among 4 shallow bowls and top with the salmon to serve.

9

Vegetarian
& Vegan Feasts

Hot Honey and Halloumi Toast

You could also serve the halloumi on smashed avocado rather than mashed peas, see GH Tip.

V

1½ standard mugful frozen peas
Finely grated zest and juice ½ lemon
1 tbsp tahini or plain yogurt
250g pack halloumi, drained
1 glug oil (vegetable, olive or sunflower are best)
1 tbsp runny honey
½ tsp dried chilli flakes, or to taste
2 thick slices bread, toasted

Hands-on time: 10 minutes, plus softening
Cooking time: about 10 minutes
Serves 2

PER SERVING 684cals, 42g protein, 38g fat
(22g saturates), 40g carbs (12g total sugars), 8g fibre

1. Tip the peas into a heatproof bowl and cover with just-boiled water from the kettle. Set aside to defrost and soften for 10 minutes. Drain well and return to the empty bowl. Roughly mash, using a potato masher or fork. Add the lemon zest and juice, tahini or yogurt and seasoning and mash again until combined. Set aside.

2. Cut the halloumi into 8 slices. Heat the oil in a medium non-stick frying pan over medium heat for 1 minute. Add the halloumi and fry for 3 minutes per side, until golden brown.

3. In a small bowl, mix the runny honey, chilli flakes and 1 tablespoon water. Pour the mixture into the halloumi pan and cook for 1 minute more, turning to coat the cheese in the sticky mixture. Remove pan from the heat.

4. Spoon the mashed peas on to the toast slices and place on 2 plates. Top with the halloumi and any sticky sauce from the pan.

GH TIP
To make smashed avocado, halve a ripe avocado, pop out the stone (by pressing on the skin behind the stone) and scoop the flesh from both sides into a bowl. Add 1 tablespoon of lemon or lime juice and some seasoning. Mash with a fork until fairly smooth.

Glass Noodle Stir-fry

Different variations of this classic dish can be found all over East Asia, from South Korea, China and Thailand to Singapore. Glass noodles can be made from a variety of starches, including sweet potato, mung bean and tapioca, and are sometimes sold as cellophane or bean thread noodles. They are readily available in most Asian shops or online.

6 tbsp light soy sauce
2 tsp dark soy sauce
1 tbsp sugar
1 tbsp sesame oil
2 garlic cloves, crushed
300g dried glass noodles
200g spinach
2 tbsp vegetable oil
1 onion, sliced
1 large carrot, peeled and julienned
150g mixed exotic mushrooms, larger ones torn
1 red pepper, deseeded and sliced
300g firm tofu, cut into 2cm slices
1 tsp sesame seeds

Hands-on time: 20 minutes
Cooking time: about 20 minutes
Serves 4

PER SERVING 561cals, 23g protein, 16g fat
(2g saturates), 78g carbs (14g total sugars), 7g fibre

1. Put the soy sauces, sugar, sesame oil, garlic and 3 tablespoons water in a medium bowl and mix well. Set aside.

2. Bring a large pan of water to the boil. Add the noodles and cook according to pack instructions. Use tongs to transfer the noodles to a colander and rinse under cold water to cool. Set aside. Bring the water back to the boil and blanch the spinach for 1 minute until wilted. Drain and cool the spinach under cold water, then squeeze thoroughly to remove excess water and set aside.

3. Heat 1 tablespoon oil in a large frying pan over medium heat and fry the onion, carrot, mushrooms and pepper for 5 minutes. Transfer to a bowl and set aside.

4. Heat the remaining 1 tablespoon oil in pan, then add the tofu and fry for 2 minutes on each side until light golden brown. Add the sauce to the pan and simmer for 1 minute, then add the noodles and stir gently but thoroughly to coat. Return the vegetables to the pan, stir well, and simmer until most of the sauce has been absorbed by the noodles. Sprinkle with sesame seeds, divide among 4 bowls and serve.

Ultimate Veggie Burger with Chopped Slaw

If you're not rushed for time, you can cover and chill the shaped patties for up to a day.

FOR THE BURGERS
1 medium sweet potato (about 150g), skin on, roughly chopped
200g chestnut mushrooms
2 tbsp olive oil
400g tin black beans, drained and rinsed
1 tbsp wholegrain mustard
Large handful parsley, finely chopped
1 medium egg
40g dried breadcrumbs

FOR THE CHOPPED COLESLAW
¼ small red cabbage, central core removed
1 medium carrot, roughly chopped
40g cornichons
Large handful parsley
150g light mayonnaise, or full-fat if you prefer
1 tbsp red or white wine vinegar
1 tbsp wholegrain mustard

TO SERVE
4 burger buns, split and toasted
2 tomatoes, sliced

Hands-on time: 30 minutes, plus cooling
Cooking time: about 15 minutes
Makes 4 burgers

PER BURGER (with 2tbsp coleslaw) 558cals, 18g protein, 23g fat (3g saturates), 64g carbs (10g total sugars), 10g fibre

1. For the burgers, in a food processor whizz the sweet potato until finely chopped (alternatively, coarsely grate by hand). Add the mushrooms and whizz until finely chopped (or you can do this by hand).

2. Heat 1 tablespoon oil in a large non-stick frying pan over high heat. Scrape in the vegetable mixture. Cook, stirring occasionally, for 5 minutes. Tip into a bowl and leave to cool for 5 minutes.

3. Meanwhile, pulse the black beans in the food processor until roughly chopped. Add to the mushroom bowl with the remaining burger ingredients (except the oil) and plenty of seasoning. Mix well, then shape and squeeze into 4 flattened patties.

4. Wipe the frying pan clean and heat the remaining 1 tablespoon olive oil over medium heat. Fry the patties for 10 minutes, turning halfway through, or until golden and piping hot throughout.

5. Meanwhile, make the chopped coleslaw. Wipe the food processor clean. Add the cabbage, carrot, cornichons and parsley, then pulse until finely chopped. Alternatively, you can finely shred the ingredients with the processor attachment, or by hand. Tip into a bowl and mix in the mayonnaise, vinegar, mustard and some seasoning.

6. Assemble the burgers in toasted buns, topped with sliced tomato and some coleslaw. Serve with the remaining coleslaw.

Smoky Mushroom Tacos

These work equally well in soft mini tortillas or crisp shells, so use whichever you prefer. To make prep time even quicker, you could replace the lime cream with shop-bought guacamole, checking it's suitable for vegans if necessary, jazzed up with extra lime juice.

VN

FOR THE TOPPINGS
½ red onion, finely sliced
Juice 2 limes
1 avocado, peeled, destoned and roughly chopped
2 tbsp vegan crème fraîche alternative
Handful coriander, leaves and stalks separated

FOR THE TACOS
1 tbsp vegetable oil
300g mini portabello (portabellini) mushrooms, thickly sliced
50g walnuts, finely chopped
1 garlic clove, crushed
2½ tbsp chipotle chilli paste
1½ tsp ground cumin
1 tsp sweet smoked paprika
60g sweetcorn (tinned or frozen, defrosted if frozen)
8 mini soft tortilla wraps or crunchy taco shells

Hands-on time: 20 minutes
Cooking time: about 10 minutes
Makes 8 tacos

PER TACO 196cals, 5g protein, 12g fat (2g saturates), 16g carbs (3g total sugars), 3g fibre

1. First make the toppings. In a small bowl, mix the onion, ½ the lime juice and a pinch of salt. Set aside to pickle until needed.

2. For the lime cream, whizz the avocado, crème fraîche alternative, remaining lime juice, coriander stalks and some salt in the small bowl of a food processor or blender until smooth and thick. Scrape into a serving bowl, cover and chill until needed.

3. For the tacos, heat the oil in a large frying pan over high heat and cook the mushrooms for 2–3 minutes, stirring occasionally, until slightly softened. Add the walnuts and garlic and fry for 1 minute, then stir in the chipotle paste, cumin, paprika and 2 tablespoons water. Bubble for 1–2 minutes, then remove from the heat and stir in the sweetcorn.

4. To serve, warm the tortillas or taco shells following pack instructions and drain the onions. Divide the mushrooms between the tortillas/tacos, then spoon over a little of the lime cream and finish with the pickled onions and coriander leaves. Serve with the remaining lime cream for spooning over.

Jackfruit and Kimchi Fried Rice

If you're craving a flavour-packed meal but are short of time, look no further. You can always leave out the sriracha sauce if the heat's not for you.

200g basmati rice
2 x 400g tins young green jackfruit, drained
1–1½ tbsp sriracha, to taste, plus extra
   to drizzle (optional)
2½ tbsp soy sauce
1 tbsp sesame oil
2 garlic cloves, crushed
5cm piece fresh root ginger, peeled and grated
3 pak choi, thickly shredded
8 tbsp (160g) jarred vegan kimchi, plus extra to garnish
4 spring onions, finely sliced
2 tsp toasted sesame seeds
Large handful coriander, roughly chopped

Hands-on time: 15 minutes
Cooking time: about 15 minutes
Serves 4

PER SERVING 386cals, 7g protein, 5g fat
(1g saturates), 76g carbs (34g total sugars), 3g fibre

1. Cook the rice according to the pack instructions. Drain well and set aside.

2. Meanwhile, drain the jackfruit and rinse well under cold running water. Using your hands, shred the fruit pieces on to clean kitchen paper and lightly pat dry. Put the jackfruit into a bowl and mix in the sriracha and half the soy sauce.

3. Heat the oil in a large non-stick frying pan over high heat. Add the garlic and ginger, fry for 2 minutes, then add the jackfruit mixture and fry for 5–7 minutes, stirring regularly, until caramelised and sticky.

4. Add the pak choi and stir-fry for 3–4 minutes, until the stalks have softened slightly. Add the kimchi, fry for 30 seconds, then stir in the cooked rice and remaining soy sauce and heat until piping hot.

5. Check the seasoning and divide among 4 bowls. Garnish with spring onions, sesame seeds, coriander and extra kimchi. Serve drizzled with extra sriracha, if you like.

GH TIP
You can use scrambled tofu instead of jackfruit, if you like.

Tempeh Goodness Bowl

Made from fermented soybeans and pressed into a block, tempeh is a rich source of plant-based protein with an earthy, mushroom-like flavour. However, you can use a firm tofu for this recipe, if you prefer. We've paired it with seasonal British veg.

FOR THE DRESSING
2 tbsp soy sauce
2 tbsp rice wine vinegar
2 tbsp maple syrup
2 tbsp sriracha
2 tbsp sesame oil
2 tbsp tahini

FOR THE BOWL
1 tbsp vegetable oil
300g tempeh, cut into 2cm pieces
150g spring greens or Swiss chard, finely sliced
2 x 250g pouches microwave brown rice
3 carrots, peeled and grated
100g radishes, trimmed and finely sliced
200g broad beans (podded weight), skins removed

Hands-on time: 25 minutes
Cooking time: about 15 minutes
Serves 4

PER SERVING 543cals, 26g protein, 20g fat
(2g saturates), 57g carbs (16g total sugars), 15g fibre

1. For the dressing, in a small bowl, whisk the soy sauce, rice wine vinegar, maple syrup, sriracha and sesame oil until combined. Spoon 2 tablespoons of the dressing into a large bowl. Whisk the tahini into the small bowl of dressing and set aside.

2. Next, heat the vegetable oil in a large non-stick frying pan over medium heat. Fry the tempeh until crispy on all sides, about 10 minutes (see GH TIP). Remove to the large bowl and toss in the 2 tablespoons of dressing to coat.

3. Return the pan to the heat and fry the spring greens/chard for 3–5 minutes, until just tender. Meanwhile, reheat the rice according to the pack instructions and divide among 4 bowls.

4. Top the rice with the tempeh, fried greens, carrots, radishes and broad beans. Drizzle over the tahini dressing and serve.

GH TIP
If you'd prefer not to fry the tempeh, toss it in the oil and roast in an oven preheated to 200°C (180°C fan) mark 6 for 15 minutes, turning once.

Asparagus Orzotto with Watercress Pesto

Pine nuts are a classic choice for creating a pesto, but you
could use blanched almonds or hazelnuts instead.

FOR THE ORZOTTO
25g butter
1 onion, finely chopped
2 garlic cloves, crushed
400g orzo
1 litre hot vegetable stock
500g asparagus, ends trimmed and roughly chopped
50g vegetarian Italian-style hard cheese, finely grated

FOR THE PESTO
75g watercress
Small handful basil
25g pine nuts, toasted
25g vegetarian Italian-style hard cheese, finely grated
1 garlic clove, crushed
3 tbsp olive oil
Finely grated zest and juice ½ lemon

Hands-on time: 15 minutes
Cooking time: about 20 minutes
Serves 4

PER SERVING 619cals, 24g protein, 22g fat
(9g saturates), 78g carbs (7g total sugars), 9g fibre

1. For the orzotto, melt the butter in a large, deep
   non-stick frying pan over medium heat and cook
   the onion for 5 minutes, until softened.

2. Stir in the garlic, orzo and some salt and pepper,
   until coated in the butter. Pour in the stock.
   Bring to the boil and bubble for 8–10 minutes,
   stirring occasionally and adding the asparagus
   for the final 4 minutes, until the orzo is tender.
   Remove from the heat, stir in the cheese and
   check the seasoning.

3. Meanwhile, in the small bowl of a food processor,
   whizz all the pesto ingredients with some
   seasoning until fairly smooth and combined.

4. Divide the orzotto among 4 bowls and swirl
   through the pesto to serve.

Greens Mac 'n' Cheese

Blending the sauce creates a silky-smooth green béchamel
for this veg-packed version of the classic. Topping with
breadcrumbs adds great crunch.

200g broccoli florets
300g macaroni pasta
100g frozen chopped spinach
250g ready-made béchamel
150g Cheddar, coarsely grated
25g dried breadcrumbs

Hands-on time: 20 minutes
Cooking time: about 30 minutes
Serves 4

PER SERVING 555cals, 25g protein, 21g fat
(12g saturates), 63g carbs (5g total sugars), 6g fibre

1. Bring a large pan of salted water to the boil and
   cook the broccoli for 4 minutes, or until tender.
   Using a slotted spoon, transfer the broccoli to
   a high-speed blender.

2. Cook the pasta in the boiling water according
   to pack instructions. Drain well and return to
   the empty pan.

3. Preheat oven to 200°C (180°C fan) mark 6.
   Meanwhile, add the frozen spinach to the
   blender with 100ml water, 100g béchamel,
   75g Cheddar and some seasoning. Whizz until
   smooth. Scrape into the pasta pan, then add the
   remaining 150g béchamel and stir to combine.
   Transfer to a 1.5 litre ovenproof serving dish.

4. In a small bowl, mix the breadcrumbs with the
   remaining 75g Cheddar and some seasoning.
   Scatter over the pasta. Cook in the oven for
   10 minutes.

5. Preheat grill to high (if yours takes a while
   to get hot, remove the dish from the oven while
   preheating). Cook for 3 minutes, or until golden
   and bubbling.

Tofu, Kale and Mixed Grains Stir-fry

Smoked tofu adds lovely flavour to this dish but use plain firm tofu if you can't get hold of it.

2 x 225g packs smoked firm tofu
2 tbsp cornflour
2 tbsp vegetable oil
2 spring onions, finely sliced
125g kale (stalks discarded), leaves roughly chopped (see GH TIP)
2 x 250g pouches mixed grains

FOR THE DRESSING
1 red chilli, deseeded and finely chopped, plus extra (optional), to serve
2 tbsp soy sauce or tamari
75g crunchy peanut butter
2 tbsp maple syrup

Hands-on time: 20 minutes
Cooking time: about 15 minutes
Serves 4

PER SERVING 639cals, 30g protein, 33g fat
(6g saturates), 50g carbs (11g total sugars), 9g fibre

1. For the stir-fry, pat the tofu dry with kitchen paper, then cut into rough 2cm cubes. Toss in a bowl with the cornflour and plenty of seasoning.

2. Heat 1 tablespoon oil in a wok or large, deep frying pan over medium-high heat and fry the tofu for 5 minutes, turning regularly, until golden all over. Remove to a plate and set aside.

3. Add the remaining 1 tablespoon oil to the wok/pan and decrease heat to medium. Add the spring onions and kale, then cook for 5 minutes, stirring occasionally, until the kale is starting to soften. Add the grains and cook for 2 minutes, until piping hot and the kale is tender.

4. Meanwhile, make the dressing. In a small bowl, whisk all the ingredients and 4 tablespoons water. Add to the wok/pan, along with the tofu, and gently mix to combine and heat through.

5. Sprinkle over extra chilli, if using, and serve.

GH TIP
You can swap the kale for shredded spring greens, or stir in spinach until wilted.

Moroccan-style Pulled Mushrooms

If you can't get hold of oyster mushrooms, use 600g chestnut mushrooms instead.

About 400g pack firm or extra-firm tofu
400g oyster mushrooms
3 tbsp olive oil
2 tsp ground cumin
2 tsp ground coriander
2 tsp smoked paprika (hot or sweet)
2 tsp ground cinnamon
2 red onions, finely sliced
3 garlic cloves, crushed
200g passata

Hands-on time: 25 minutes
Cooking time: about 35 minutes
Serves 6

PER SERVING 176cals, 11g protein, 11g fat
(2g saturates), 7g carbs (5g total sugars), 4g fibre

1. Preheat grill to high. Coarsely grate the tofu, then, using kitchen paper or a clean tea towel, pat it dry. Tear the mushrooms into thin strips.

2. Put the mushrooms and tofu on a large baking tray (the type that slots into the oven racks) and spread them out as much as possible. Grill for 5–10 minutes, turning halfway through, or until the mushrooms look dry.

3. Meanwhile, in a small bowl, mix 2 tablespoons oil and the spices. Add to the tofu mixture and toss to coat. Spread out again and return to the grill for 10–15 minutes, turning occasionally, or until cooked through and beginning to char.

4. Meanwhile, heat the remaining 1 tablespoon oil in a large pan over medium heat. Cook the onions for 10 minutes, until slightly softened. Add the garlic and cook for 1 minute, until fragrant. Stir in the tofu mixture, passata, 300ml water and plenty of seasoning. Bring to the boil and bubble for 5 minutes, or until thick and glossy.

5. Transfer to a warmed serving dish and serve.

GET AHEAD
Prepare to end of step 4 up to a day ahead. Cool, cover and chill. To serve, reheat gently in a pan, stirring occasionally, until piping hot.

Curried Lentils
with Coconut Flatbreads

If you don't need the flatbreads to be vegan, you can replace the coconut yogurt alternative with a dairy version.

VN

FOR THE FLATBREADS
200g self-raising flour, plus extra to dust
200g dairy-free coconut yogurt alternative, plus extra
   to serve (optional)

FOR THE CURRIED LENTILS
1 tbsp vegetable oil
1 onion, finely chopped
4 garlic cloves, crushed
5cm piece fresh root ginger, peeled and grated
2 tsp each ground cumin and ground coriander
1 tsp ground turmeric
1 tsp black mustard seeds
1–2 green chillies, to taste, deseeded and finely chopped
2 x 400g tins green lentils, drained and rinsed
200ml vegetable stock
400ml tin coconut milk
100g baby spinach, roughly chopped
Small handful coriander, roughly chopped

Hands-on time: 25 minutes
Cooking time: about 25 minutes
Serves 4

PER SERVING 735cals, 23g protein, 29g fat
(20g saturates), 87g carbs (12g total sugars),
0.6g fibre

1. For the flatbreads, in a medium bowl, mix the flour, a pinch of fine salt and the coconut yogurt alternative to make a dough. Tip on to a floured work surface and knead for 1 minute, then cover with the empty upturned bowl and leave to rest.

2. For the curried lentils, heat the oil in a large pan over medium heat and fry the onion and a pinch of salt for 5 minutes, until starting to soften. Stir in the garlic, ginger, ground spices, mustard seeds and chilli(es), and cook for 1 minute, until fragrant.

3. Add the lentils, stock and coconut milk to the onion pan and bring to the boil. Bubble for 5 minutes to reduce slightly.

4. Meanwhile, divide the rested dough in half. Lightly flour a work surface and roll out each portion to a rough 20.5cm round. Heat a large frying pan (that has a lid) over medium-high heat. Add a flatbread, cover the pan with a lid and fry for 2–3 minute per side until speckled golden. Wrap the flatbread in a clean tea towel and repeat with the remaining flatbread dough. Add to the tea towel.

5. Add the spinach and half a teaspoon salt to the lentil pan and stir until the spinach wilts. Check the seasoning. Sprinkle over the coriander and serve with the flatbreads and extra coconut yogurt alternative, if using.

10

30-minute
Meals

Coca-Cola Chicken Wraps

The Coca-Cola sauce bubbles down to a lovely sticky glaze. Chicken thighs stay juicy when cooking and are a cheaper alternative to breast. The chicken mixture would also be lovely served with rice instead of in wraps.

1 small glug oil (vegetable, olive or sunflower are best)
1 red onion, halved and sliced
1 red, orange or yellow pepper, deseeded and sliced
4 skinless and boneless chicken thighs, cut into finger-size strips
330ml can Coca-Cola
2 tbsp tomato ketchup
2 tbsp soy sauce

TO SERVE
Soft tortilla wraps
Iceberg lettuce, shredded
Yogurt

Hands-on time: 10 minutes
Cooking time: about 20 minutes
Serves 2

PER SERVING (chicken mixture only) 350cals, 33g protein, 10g fat (2g saturates), 30g carbs (29g total sugars), 3g fibre

1. Heat the oil in a large, deep frying pan over medium heat for 1 minute. Add the onion, pepper and chicken and fry for a couple of minutes, stirring occasionally.

2. Add the Coca-Cola, ketchup, soy sauce and some seasoning. Turn up the heat to high and bubble until the sauce has reduced to a sticky glaze, about 15 minutes.

3. Check the seasoning and serve the chicken mixture wrapped in flour tortillas with shredded lettuce and a spoonful of yogurt.

Piri Piri Salmon
with Herby Rice

Swap the salmon for another type of fish, if you like; cod
loins or tuna steaks work particularly well.

225g white basmati and wild rice mix
350ml vegetable stock
1 garlic clove, crushed
1 tbsp sweet smoked paprika
1 tsp mild chilli powder
½ tsp ground cumin
½ tsp dried chilli flakes
½ tsp each dried oregano and dried thyme
2 tbsp olive oil
4 skinless salmon fillets (about 120g each)
Finely grated zest and juice 1 lime
Large handful coriander, roughly chopped

FOR THE SLAW
½ red cabbage, cored and finely shredded
½ red onion, finely sliced
2 tbsp Dijon mustard
250g natural yogurt
Juice 2 limes

Hands-on time: 10 minutes
Cooking time: about 20 minutes
Serves 4

PER SERVING 553cals, 36g protein, 20g fat
(4g saturates), 56g carbs (10g total sugars), 4g fibre

1. Preheat oven to 200°C (180°C fan) mark 6.
   Rinse the rice under cold water and drain. Add to
   a medium pan with the stock, then simmer over
   medium heat. Stir then cover with a lid. Reduce
   the heat to low and cook for 17 minutes. Remove
   from the heat and set aside with the lid on.

2. Meanwhile, mix the garlic, spices, dried herbs,
   oil and seasoning in a bowl. Put the salmon on
   a baking tray lined with baking parchment. Brush
   with the spice mix. Oven roast for 15 minutes,
   or until the salmon flakes when pressed.

3. Meanwhile, mix all the slaw ingredients and
   season well.

4. Uncover the rice, sprinkle over the lime zest,
   juice and coriander and fork through to mix.
   Divide among 4 plates and serve with the
   salmon and slaw.

Hot and Sour Pork Broth

A clean and sprightly broth that is ideal for a light supper. Replace the pork with the same weight of skinless chicken breast, if you prefer.

200g rice noodles
1 tbsp groundnut or vegetable oil
125g shiitake mushrooms, sliced
2 garlic cloves, finely sliced
5cm piece fresh root ginger, cut into matchsticks
2 litres chicken stock
350g pork fillet, cut into strips
150g sugar snap peas, sliced lengthways
2 tbsp rice vinegar
2 tbsp soy sauce
1–2 tsp sriracha, to taste

TO GARNISH
Spring onions, finely sliced
Fresh coriander, chopped
Red chilli, finely sliced (optional)

Hands-on time: 15 minutes
Cooking time: about 15 minutes
Serves 4

PER SERVING 511cals, 44g protein, 9g fat
(2g saturates), 62g carbs (4g total sugars), 1g fibre

1. Put the noodles in a heatproof bowl and cover with hot water. Leave to soak until pliable – about 10 minutes.

2. Meanwhile, heat the oil in a large pan over high heat and fry mushrooms for 2–3 minutes until lightly golden. Add the garlic and ginger and cook for 30 seconds. Add the stock and bring to the boil.

3. Meanwhile, drain the noodles. Add to the pan with the pork and sugar snap peas. Bring back to the boil and simmer for 4 minutes until pork is cooked through. Add the vinegar, soy sauce and sriracha sauce, and check the seasoning.

4. Ladle into bowls and garnish with the spring onions, coriander and chilli, if you like.

Smoky Prawn and Corn Tacos

Frozen prawns are a great standby; they're cheaper than fresh and cook from frozen in minutes. To make this dish even easier, you could swap the homemade avocado crema for a smooth shop-bought guacamole.

FOR THE TACOS
1 tbsp vegetable oil
1 red onion, finely sliced
2 garlic cloves, crushed
2 tbsp smoked paprika (sweet or hot)
2 tsp light brown soft sugar
300g frozen raw peeled prawns
150g sweetcorn, tinned or frozen
8-12 mini soft tortilla wraps, warmed

FOR THE AVOCADO CREMA
1 ripe avocado, halved and destoned
Juice 1 lime, plus extra wedges, to serve
1 garlic clove, crushed
2 tbsp soured cream
Small handful coriander, plus extra leaves (optional),
   to serve

Hands-on time: 15 minutes
Cooking time: about 15 minutes
Serves 4

PER SERVING (with 2 tortillas) 410cals, 21g protein,
16g fat (5g saturates), 44g carbs (8g total sugars),
5g fibre

1. For the tacos, heat the oil in a large frying pan over medium heat and cook the onion and a large pinch of salt for 5 minutes, until starting to soften.

2. Meanwhile, make the avocado crema. Scoop the flesh from the avocado into a bowl and add the remaining ingredients and some seasoning. Whizz with a stick blender until smooth (or finely chop the coriander and thoroughly mash all ingredients together with a fork). Set aside.

3. Add the garlic, smoked paprika and sugar to the onion pan and fry for 2 minutes. Stir in the prawns, increase the heat to medium-high and cook for 5 minutes, stirring frequently, until the prawns are opaque and cooked through. Add the sweetcorn and cook to heat through.

4. Serve the prawn mixture with warmed tortilla wraps, avocado crema, lime wedges and extra coriander, if you like.

GH TIP
We used jumbo prawns, but this would be equally tasty with small coldwater prawns.

Chicken and Mango Salad

A taste of summer on a plate, this fruity salad relies
on juicy ripe mangoes to make a smooth dressing.

(DF)

FOR THE SALAD
3 skinless chicken breasts
1 tbsp olive oil
2 ripe mangoes, destoned and finely chopped
200g cherry tomatoes, quartered
2 avocados, destoned and chopped
½ red onion, finely chopped
½ red chilli, deseeded and finely chopped
2 Little Gem lettuces, roughly chopped
100g baby spinach, roughly chopped
Small handful coriander, finely chopped

FOR THE DRESSING
Juice 1 lime
3 tbsp olive oil
1 tsp cider vinegar
1 tsp runny honey
1 tsp Dijon mustard

Hands-on time: 15 minutes
Cooking time: about 15 minutes
Serves 4

PER SERVING 457cals, 31g protein, 28g fat
(5g saturates), 17g carbs (15g total sugars), 8g fibre

GH TIP
To cook the chicken in the
oven, follow step 1, then
arrange the chicken on a
baking tray lined with baking
parchment. Preheat oven to
200°C (180°C fan) mark 6 and
cook for 15 minutes, or until
cooked through.

1. For the salad, working 1 at a time, put the
   chicken breasts between 2 sheets of baking
   parchment and bash with a rolling pin to flatten
   to an even 5mm thickness. Rub the oil over
   each flattened breast and season.

2. Heat a large griddle or frying pan over high
   heat. Griddle or fry the chicken (in batches if
   needed) for 2–3 minutes per side, or until cooked
   through (see GH TIP).

3. Meanwhile, put three-quarters of the mango into
   a large bowl. Add the cherry tomatoes, avocados,
   onion, chilli, Little Gem, spinach and coriander
   and gently toss to combine.

4. For the dressing, in the small bowl of a food
   processor or a high-speed blender, whizz the
   remaining mango with all the dressing
   ingredients and some seasoning until smooth.

5. Slice the chicken and add to the bowl along
   with the dressing. Toss to combine. Transfer to
   a platter and serve.

Spinach and Feta Lasagne

If your lasagne doesn't need to be vegetarian, you can use
Parmesan instead of Italian-style hard cheese.

200g baby spinach
200g feta
250g ricotta
100g vegetarian Italian-style hard cheese, grated
250g fresh lasagne sheets
200g cherry tomatoes, halved

Hands-on time: 10 minutes
Cooking time: about 20 minutes
Serves 4

PER SERVING 524cals, 31g protein, 27g fat
(17g saturates), 38g carbs (5g total sugars), 3g fibre

1. Preheat oven to 200°C (180°C fan) mark 6.
   Put the spinach into a large heatproof bowl,
   then cover with just-boiled water from the kettle.
   Leave for 1 minute, then drain and cool under
   cold running water. Rinse and drain again. Lift
   up handfuls and squeeze out as much excess
   liquid as you can. Return the spinach to the
   empty bowl.

2. In a food processor, whizz the feta, ricotta and
   a little seasoning until smooth and combined.
   Alternatively, mash with a fork in a medium
   bowl until combined. Add the mixture to the
   spinach bowl with 75g of the hard cheese.
   Mix to combine.

3. Arrange a third of the lasagne sheets in the base
   of a roughly 22 x 28cm ovenproof serving dish.
   Top with a third of the ricotta mix, spreading to
   level. Add half the tomatoes. Repeat the layers
   twice more, finishing with the ricotta mixture.
   Sprinkle over the remaining 25g hard cheese.

4. Cook in the oven for 20 minutes, or until the
   lasagne is golden and bubbling. Serve with
   a crisp green salad, if you like.

Sausage and Fennel Pasta

A hit of fennel (boosted by fennel seeds) helps add summer freshness to this midweek winner.

275g pasta (we used riccioli)
1 large fennel bulb (about 400g)
1 tbsp olive oil
4 pork sausages
2 garlic cloves, crushed
1 tsp fennel seeds
2 tsp wholegrain mustard
200ml chicken stock or water
100g cream cheese
50g Parmesan, grated, plus extra to serve

Hands-on time: 10 minutes
Cooking time: about 20 minutes
Serves 4

PER SERVING 579cals, 27g protein, 27g fat (12g saturates), 53g carbs (4g total sugars), 7g fibre

1. Bring a large pan of salted water to the boil and cook the pasta according to pack instructions. Drain. Meanwhile, halve the fennel lengthways and remove and discard the core. Finely slice the bulb, reserving any fronds for garnish.

2. Heat the oil in a large deep frying pan over medium heat. Add the fennel and fry for 10 minutes, until softened. Meanwhile, squeeze the sausages out of their skins (or slit and peel off the skins) and discard the skins.

3. Tip the fennel into a bowl. Return the pan to the heat. Add the sausagemeat in bite-size pieces and fry for 5–7 minutes, until browned and cooked through. Add the garlic, fennel seeds and mustard and cook for 1 minute.

4. Return the fennel to the pan with the stock or water, cream cheese, some salt and plenty of freshly ground black pepper. Heat until melted and combined. Toss through the drained pasta and Parmesan. Check seasoning and serve, sprinkled with any reserved fennel fronds and extra Parmesan, if you like.

Prawn Moilee Curry

A light and fragrant south Indian-style curry, perfect for a warm summer's evening.

1 tbsp vegetable oil
2 tsp black mustard seeds
10 dried curry leaves, or use 5 fresh leaves
1 large onion, finely sliced
3 garlic cloves, crushed
5cm piece fresh root ginger, peeled and finely grated
2–3 green chillies, deseeded and finely chopped
1 tsp turmeric
600ml full-fat or light coconut milk
3 medium tomatoes, roughly chopped
450g raw peeled king prawns
Juice ½ lemon

Hands-on time: 5 minutes
Cooking time: about 25 minutes
Serves 4

PER SERVING (with light coconut milk) 273cals, 23g protein, 16g fat (10g saturates), 9g carbs (9g total sugars), 2g fibre

1. Heat the oil in a large deep pan over medium heat. Add the mustard seeds and curry leaves and cook for 30 seconds, until the seeds are popping. Add the onion and a pinch of salt and cook for 10 minutes, until softened.

2. Stir in the garlic, ginger, chillies, turmeric and 1 tablespoon water and cook for 2 minutes, until fragrant. Stir in the coconut milk, tomatoes and 200ml water. Bring to the boil and bubble for 5 minutes, until slightly reduced.

3. Add the prawns and cook for 5 minutes, or until the prawns are opaque and cooked through. Stir in the lemon juice and check the seasoning. Serve with parathas or white rice, if you like.

Chicken
Puttanesca

This pasta dish traditionally makes the most of
storecupboard ingredients — we've added chicken breasts
to make it more substantial.

4 skin-on chicken breasts
1 tbsp olive oil
3 anchovy fillets, chopped
3 garlic cloves, crushed
1 tsp dried chilli flakes
100g black olives, de-stoned
2 x 400g tins chopped tomatoes
Small bunch basil, leaves picked, stalks chopped
300g fresh tagliatelle or spaghetti
Parmesan shavings, to serve

Hands-on time: 5 minutes
Cooking time: about 25 minutes
Serves 4

PER SERVING 335cals, 34g protein, 16g fat
(4g saturates), 11g carbs (10g total sugars), 4g fibre

1. In a casserole over a medium heat, fry the
   chicken, skin-side down, in the olive oil for
   8 minutes until brown. With a slotted spoon,
   remove to a plate and set aside.

2. Add the anchovies, garlic and chilli and fry
   for 15 seconds. Stir in the olives and tomatoes,
   basil stalks and half the leaves.

3. Add 200ml boiling water. Nestle the chicken
   into the sauce (skin-side up), cover and simmer
   for 15 minutes until chicken is cooked.

4. Meanwhile, in a large pan of salted water,
   cook the pasta according to pack instructions.
   Drain, then divide among 4 plates with the
   chicken and sauce. Scatter over the Parmesan
   shavings and remaining basil leaves to serve.

11

Storecupboard Saviours

Speedy Lentil and Antipasti Frittata

Try our super-easy and nutritious frittata, filled with anything you might have in your storecupboard or fridge. Ours has lentils, artichokes and olives, but use what you have and get creative!

10 medium eggs
1 tbsp olive oil
250g pack ready-to-eat lentils
200g antipasti mix (we used chargrilled vegetables and olives)
Large handful parsley, roughly chopped

Hands-on time: 15 minutes
Cooking time: about 10 minutes
Serves 4

PER SERVING 351cals, 24g protein, 21g fat (5g saturates), 14g carbs (2g total sugars), 6g fibre

1. Preheat grill to medium. Crack the eggs into a large jug and beat with some seasoning.

2. Heat the oil in a 23cm non-stick ovenproof frying pan over a medium heat and add the eggs. Top with the lentils and move the mixture around a little to fluff up the eggs, then leave to cook for a couple of minutes until the base is set. Scatter over the antipasti and the parsley.

3. Grill for 5 minutes, until cooked through (check the egg is set in the middle). Allow to sit for 2 minutes, then slide on to a board. Serve with a crisp green salad, if you like.

Gnocchi Cacio e Pepe

This dish is traditionally made with spaghetti, but it's equally delicious with gnocchi. It's so quick and easy to make, it'll become a weekly staple.

V

800g gnocchi
75g butter
1½ tsp freshly ground black pepper
50g vegetarian Italian-style hard cheese (or use Pecorino Romano), at room temperature, finely grated, plus extra (optional) to serve

Hands-on time: 10 minutes
Cooking time: about 10 minutes
Serves 4

PER SERVING 490cals, 12g protein, 20g fat (12g saturates), 64g carbs (1g total sugars), 4g fibre

1. Bring a large pan of salted water to the boil and cook the gnocchi until they bob to the surface.

2. Meanwhile, melt the butter in a large non-stick frying pan over medium heat. When foaming, add the black pepper and cook for 1 minute, until fragrant.

3. Add a ladleful of the gnocchi cooking water (about 75ml) to the pan and toss with the butter to emulsify. Next, using a slotted spoon, add the gnocchi to the pan, followed by the cheese. Toss to melt and combine.

4. Divide among 4 bowls and serve immediately with extra cheese, if you like.

GH TIP
Make sure your cheese is finely grated and at room temperature to ensure the smoothest sauce results.

Tuna and Sweetcorn Fritters

Raid your pantry shelves for this easy, low-key supper.
You could also serve the fritters topped with a fried egg
instead of the mayo.

FOR THE FRITTERS
4 heaped tbsp self-raising flour
2 medium eggs
3 heaped tbsp sweet chilli sauce
198g tin sweetcorn, drained
2 spring onions, finely chopped
145g tin tuna chunks, drained
1 glug oil (vegetable, olive or sunflower are best), plus
   extra to fry, if needed

FOR THE CHILLI MAYO
4 tbsp mayonnaise
2 tbsp sweet chilli sauce

Hands-on time: 30 minutes
Cooking time: about 15 minutes
Serves 2

PER SERVING 691cals, 26g protein, 38g fat
(5g saturates), 59g carbs (26g total sugars), 4g fibre

1. For the fritters, in a medium bowl mix the flour, eggs and the 3 tablespoons of sweet chilli sauce until combined. Mix in the sweetcorn, spring onions, tuna and plenty of seasoning.

2. Heat the oil in a large non-stick frying pan over medium heat for 1 minute. Using a cutlery spoon, add heaped double-spoonfuls of the fritter mixture to the pan, spacing them apart (you want 6 fritters, but may need to do this in batches). Flatten the fritters in the pan a little with the back of the spoon. Cook for 3–4 minutes, or until the bases are golden, then flip and cook for 3–4 minutes more to cook through. Lift out of the pan on to a plate.

3. Cook any remaining batter into fritters, adding a little extra oil first, if needed. Meanwhile, in a small bowl mix the chilli mayo ingredients with some seasoning.

4. Divide the fritters between 2 plates and serve with the chilli mayo.

Roasted Tomato
and Basil Oven Risotto

No need to spend all that time stirring to create a risotto – let the oven do the work for you! If you can't find the mozzarella pearls, chop up some regular mozzarella.

2 tbsp olive oil
1 fat garlic clove, crushed
400g risotto rice
2 x 600g tubs fresh tomato and basil soup
275g cherry tomatoes on the vine
40g vegetarian Italian-style hard cheese (or use
   Parmesan), finely grated
125–150g mozzarella pearls or mozzarella cherries

Hands-on time: 10 minutes
Cooking time: about 35 minutes
Serves 4

PER SERVING 671cals, 20g protein, 22g fat
(10g saturates), 96g carbs (12g total sugars), 7g fibre

1. Preheat oven to 200°C (180°C fan) mark 6. Heat 1½ tablespoons of the oil in a large, ovenproof casserole (that has a lid) over medium heat. Add the garlic and rice, and cook, stirring, for 1 minute. Pour in the soup, season and bring to a simmer, stirring. Cover with a lid and cook in the oven for 20 minutes.

2. Meanwhile, put the tomatoes on a small baking tray, drizzle with the remaining oil and season. Cook in the oven for 10–15 minutes until starting to split and soften.

3. Remove the risotto from the oven, stir in most of the hard cheese and all of the mozzarella. Re-cover with the lid and return to the oven for 10 minutes, until the rice is tender and the soup has been absorbed.

4. Sprinkle over the remaining cheese and top with the roasted tomatoes to serve.

Peanut Butter Noodles with Thai Beans

This protein-packed meal is made using just jar and packet ingredients. Perfect for when fresh supplies are running low.

250g egg noodles
4 tbsp peanut butter
2 tbsp soy sauce
Pinch dried chilli flakes
1 tbsp sweet chilli sauce, plus extra to drizzle
½ tbsp white wine vinegar
1 tbsp toasted sesame oil
4 tbsp Thai green curry paste
2 x 400g tins mixed beans, drained and rinsed
Dried coriander, to garnish (optional)

Hands-on time: 10 minutes
Cooking time: about 10 minutes
Serves 4

PER SERVING 558cals, 24g protein, 22g fat
(4g saturates), 64g carbs (4g total sugars), 6g fibre

1. Bring a pan of water to the boil and cook the egg noodles according to the pack instructions. Meanwhile, in a small bowl, whisk together the peanut butter, soy sauce, chilli flakes, sweet chilli sauce and vinegar (it will be thick).

2. In a small frying pan, heat the sesame oil, curry paste and 50ml water for 1 minute. Stir in the mixed beans and heat through.

3. Drain the noodles, reserving a cupful of cooking water. Return the noodles to the empty pan with the peanut sauce and enough reserved cooking water to thin to a loose sauce consistency. Serve topped with the Thai beans, an extra drizzle of sweet chilli sauce and a sprinkle of dried coriander, if you like.

Shakshuka

We've added pulses to bulk up this Middle Eastern breakfast dish. Make sure your eggs are the freshest possible so they poach neatly.

2 tbsp olive oil
1 onion, chopped
1 each red and green pepper, deseeded and chopped
2 garlic cloves, crushed
2 tbsp harissa paste
1 tbsp tomato purée
950g ripe tomatoes, roughly chopped
½ tsp sugar
2 tsp red wine vinegar
400g tin chickpeas, drained and rinsed
4 large eggs

Hands-on time: 15 minutes
Cooking time: about 45 minutes
Serves 4

PER SERVING 319cals, 15g protein, 15g fat (3g saturates), 26g carbs (15g total sugars), 9g fibre

1. In a large frying pan (one with a lid), heat the oil and gently fry the onion and peppers until beginning to soften, about 15 minutes.

2. Add the garlic, harissa paste and tomato purée, stirring for 1 minute. Add the tomatoes, sugar, vinegar and chickpeas. Reduce the heat and simmer gently for 15 minutes until the tomatoes are tender and pulpy.

3. Make 4 indentations in the sauce and crack an egg into each. Spread the egg whites into the sauce slightly but don't burst the yolks.

4. Cover the pan and simmer gently for 15 minutes, or until the egg whites are cooked but the yolks are still runny. Serve.

Sardine Bolognese

Sardines add a super savoury note and flavour to this
popular pasta dish, without pushing up the price.

350g spaghetti
1 tbsp olive oil
1 onion, finely sliced
2 carrots, finely chopped
3 celery sticks, finely chopped
200g mushrooms, roughly chopped
2 garlic cloves, crushed
2 x 120g tins sardines in tomato sauce
2 x 400g tins chopped tomatoes
Pinch sugar
Large handful parsley, roughly chopped

Hands-on time: 25 minutes
Cooking time: about 15 minutes
Serves 4

PER SERVING 527cals, 27g protein, 11g fat
(2g saturates), 76g carbs (15g total sugars), 9g fibre

1. Bring a large pan of water to the boil. Add
   the spaghetti to the boiling water and cook
   according to the pack instructions.

2. Meanwhile, heat the oil in a large, deep frying
   pan and gently fry the onion, carrots and celery
   for 5 minutes until softened. Turn up the heat
   to medium high and add the mushrooms. Fry,
   stirring occasionally, until the mushrooms are
   tender and there is barely any liquid in the pan.
   Add the garlic and fry for 1 minute more.

3. Add the contents of the sardine tins, together
   with the tinned tomatoes and sugar. Bring to
   the boil, then reduce the heat to medium and
   bubble for 5 minutes, stirring occasionally to
   break up the sardines.

4. When the pasta is cooked to your liking, drain
   well. Divide among 4 pasta bowls, top with the
   sardine Bolognese and sprinkle with the
   chopped parsley to serve.

Salmon Fishcakes with Minted Mashed Peas

Wonderfully versatile, these fishcakes are made with tinned salmon for an economical midweek meal.

500g floury potatoes, cut into about 2cm chunks
2 x 213g tins red salmon, drained
3 tbsp capers, chopped
3 spring onions, chopped
Zest and juice 1 lemon
50g plain flour
1 egg, beaten
100g dried breadcrumbs – we used panko
50g unsalted butter
700g frozen peas
Small bunch mint, finely chopped
5-6 tbsp sunflower oil, to shallow fry

Hands-on time: 15 minutes
Cooking time: about 40 minutes
Serves 4

PER SERVING 784cals, 41g protein, 37g fat
(11g saturates), 65g carbs (7g total sugars), 15g fibre

1. Fill a medium pan with cold water and bring the potato chunks to the boil. Simmer for 20 minutes or until soft. Drain, return to the pan and mash.

2. Mix the mashed potatoes with the salmon, capers, spring onions and lemon zest and juice. Season to taste.

3. Divide the mixture into 8 patties. Set up 3 shallow bowls: 1 with flour, 1 with beaten egg and 1 with breadcrumbs. Dip each fishcake into the flour, then egg, then breadcrumbs. Chill.

4. Meanwhile, make the pea mash. Melt the butter in a large frying pan over medium heat, add the peas and cook for about 5 minutes. Transfer to a food processor and pulse until coarsely puréed, then stir in the mint and season to taste. (Alternatively, mash the peas by hand.)

5. Return the frying pan to the heat, add the oil and fry the fishcakes until browned and warmed through, about 5 minutes each side. You may need to do this in batches. Serve with minted mashed peas and lemon wedges, if you like.

Packet Noodles with Smacked Cucumber

You can use any packet of instant ramen noodles here – look out for supermarket-own brands as they're usually cheaper. If you have it in the cupboard, add 1 teaspoon sesame oil to the dressing for an extra boost of flavour.

2 x 90g chicken flavour packet noodles
2 tbsp soy sauce
1 tbsp white wine vinegar
1 tsp hot sauce or chilli oil, plus optional extra to serve
1 garlic clove, peeled and finely chopped or crushed
1 tsp sugar
1 medium cucumber, ends trimmed

Hands-on time: 15 minutes
Serves 2

PER SERVING 492cals, 11g protein, 21g fat (9g saturates), 63g carbs (7g total sugars), 5g fibre

1. Empty the noodles into a large heatproof bowl and sprinkle in the seasoning from the sachets. Pour in just-boiled water from the kettle to just cover the noodles, making sure they are submerged. Set aside to soften for 5 minutes, or until just cooked.

2. Meanwhile, in a separate large bowl mix the soy sauce, vinegar, hot sauce or chilli oil, the garlic and sugar until combined.

3. Put the cucumber on a chopping board, place a large, wide knife over it sideways (as if you are bashing a garlic clove) and bash down on the knife, all along the cucumber, to squash it slightly. You can also use a rolling pin to do this. Next, halve the cucumber lengthways, then again, so you have 4 long pieces. Cut the lengths into rough 1cm chunks. Add to the dressing bowl and toss to coat.

4. Drain the noodles, add to the cucumber bowl and toss to coat. Divide between 2 bowls and serve with extra hot sauce or chilli oil, if you like.

Peach Crumble

This crumble, made purely from storecupboard ingredients, is sure to be a hit with vegans and non-vegans alike. Serve with dairy or non-dairy cream if you'd like to elevate it slightly.

FOR THE FILLING
3 x 410g tins peach slices, drained and rinsed
½ tsp ground cinnamon
1 tbsp dark brown soft sugar

FOR THE CRUMBLE
100g porridge oats
3 tbsp desiccated coconut
50g golden syrup
50ml vegetable oil

Hands-on time: 10 minutes
Cooking time: about 45 minutes
Serves 4

PER SERVING 347cals, 4g protein, 17g fat (7g saturates), 43g carbs (28g total sugars), 5g fibre

1. Preheat oven 200°C (180°C fan) mark 6. For the filling, combine all the ingredients in a medium pan, cover and cook over medium heat for 15 minutes, stirring occasionally, or until the peaches are beginning to break down.

2. Remove the lid and continue to cook the filling for 5 minutes, until most of the liquid has evaporated. Scrape the mixture into a shallow 1 litre ovenproof serving dish.

3. In a medium bowl, mix together the crumble ingredients and scatter over the peaches. Bake in the oven for 20-25 minutes until the crumble is golden.

4. Serve hot, with vegan cream or ice cream, if you like (or dairy alternatives, if preferred).

12

From the
Freezer

Curried Parsnip Soup

Parsnips make a wonderfully rich and warming soup, especially when paired with mellow spices. To make this vegan, use vegan stock and swap the yogurt for a dairy-free coconut alternative.

V

2 tsp vegetable oil
1 large onion, finely chopped
3 celery sticks, coarsely grated
2 garlic cloves, crushed
3cm piece fresh root ginger, peeled and grated
1 tbsp mild curry powder
500g parsnips, cut into rough 2cm pieces
400g potatoes, cut into rough 2cm pieces
1.25 litres hot vegetable stock
4 tbsp natural yogurt

FOR THE SPICE OIL
5 tbsp vegetable oil
1 tbsp black/brown mustard seeds
2 tsp mild curry powder
Handful curry leaves
½ tsp dried chilli flakes (optional)

Hands-on time: 20 minutes
Cooking time: about 35 minutes
Serves 6

PER SERVING 271cals, 5g protein, 13g fat
(2g saturates), 28g carbs (9g total sugars), 8g fibre

1. For the soup, heat the oil in a large pan (that has a lid) over a low heat. Add the onion, celery and a pinch of salt, then cook gently for 10 minutes until softened. Add the garlic, ginger and curry powder and cook for 2 minutes, until fragrant.

2. Increase heat to medium-high, add the parsnips, potatoes and stock, bring to the boil, cover and bubble for 15–20 minutes, or until the vegetables are cooked through and completely tender.

3. Meanwhile, make the spice oil. Heat all the ingredients in a small pan with 1 tablespoon water over low heat, until the spices bubble and smell aromatic, about 4–5 minutes. Season with a pinch of salt and set aside.

4. Remove the soup from the heat, add the yogurt and carefully whizz in a blender until smooth.

5. Return the soup to the pan and reheat gently (if needed), thinning with a little extra water or stock if too thick. Check the seasoning. Divide among 6 bowls and top each with a generous swirl of the spice oil.

FREEZE AHEAD
Complete to end of step 4. Cool, transfer to a freezer-safe container and freeze for up to 3 months. Store spice oil in a jar at room temperature for up to 3 months. Defrost soup in fridge overnight and complete recipe to serve.

FREEZE AHEAD
Prepare to end of step 5.
Cool completely, wrap the
dish well and freeze for up to
1 month. To serve, defrost in
the fridge overnight, unwrap
and complete the recipe.

Butter Chicken Pie

We've turned the popular curry into a tasty, naan-topped pie.
You can use plain naan for the topping or give it an extra boost
of flavour with a garlic and coriander or peshwari variety.

6 green cardamom pods
1 tsp fenugreek seeds
2 tsp cumin seeds
1 tsp turmeric
½ tsp cayenne pepper
2 garlic cloves
2.5cm piece fresh root ginger, peeled and grated
2 cinnamon sticks
100g natural yogurt
250g skinless boneless chicken thigh fillets, cut into
   bite-size pieces
25g butter
1 onion, finely chopped
400g tomatoes, roughly chopped
2 tbsp tomato purée
400g tin butter beans, drained and rinsed
150ml single cream
75g baby/young spinach

FOR THE TOPPING
150g naan bread
25g butter, melted
1 tsp cumin seeds

Hands-on time: 25 minutes, plus marinating
Cooking time: about 1 hour
Serves 6

PER SERVING 317cals, 17g protein, 16g fat
(8g saturates), 23g carbs (7g total sugars), 5g fibre

1. With a pestle and mortar, bash open the
   cardamom pods. Pick out the seeds and discard
   the husks. Add the fenugreek and cumin seeds,
   turmeric, cayenne, garlic and ginger to the
   cardamom seeds and grind to a rough paste.

2. Scrape the paste into a non-metallic bowl,
   then add the cinnamon sticks, yogurt, chicken
   and some seasoning. Mix, cover, and chill to
   marinate for at least 30 minutes (up to 24 hours).

3. Melt the butter in a large pan and gently fry
   the onion, stirring occasionally, for 15 minutes,
   until golden. Add the chicken, tomatoes, tomato
   purée, beans and cream. Bring to the boil, then
   simmer for 15 minutes until the chicken is
   cooked through and the sauce thickens.

4. Meanwhile, in a food processor, whizz the naan
   bread to chunky crumbs. Empty into a small
   bowl, then add the melted butter and 1 teaspoon
   cumin seeds. Stir to coat.

5. Preheat oven to 200°C (180°C fan) mark 6.
   Remove and discard the cinnamon sticks from
   the curry and stir through the spinach, then
   check the seasoning. Spoon into a 1.5 litre
   ovenproof serving dish. Sprinkle the
   breadcrumb mixture over the curry.

6. Cook in the oven for 30 minutes until golden
   and bubbling, covering with foil if the topping
   starts to brown too much. Serve the pie with
   peas, if you like.

Sausage and Caramelised Red Onion Tarte Tatin

This winter warmer is both comforting and impressive. It's important to rest your puff pastry at room temperature before unrolling it to prevent cracking – check the packet instructions for the recommended time, it's usually about 10 minutes.

320g sheet ready-rolled puff pastry, at room temperature
1 medium egg, beaten, to brush
1 tsp olive oil
8 chipolatas
25g butter
350g small red onions, each cut into 6 wedges through the root
75ml port or red wine
1 tsp thyme leaves, plus 4 whole sprigs, cut into pieces if large
1 tbsp light brown soft sugar
100g baby plum or cherry tomatoes

Hands-on time: 25 minutes, plus cooling
Cooking time: about 50 minutes
Serves 4

PER SERVING 463cals, 14g protein, 31g fat
(14g saturates), 27g carbs (11g total sugars), 3g fibre

1. Unroll the pastry and cut a rough circle slightly larger than a 20.5cm springform tin (roll the pastry out a little more, if needed). Slide on to a baking sheet, brush lightly with the egg, prick all over with a fork and chill until needed. Line the tin with a double layer of baking parchment, so it covers the base and comes up the sides.

2. Heat the oil in a large, non-stick frying pan over medium heat, add the chipolatas and brown all over. Remove to a plate. Preheat oven to 200°C (180°C fan) mark 6.

3. Add the butter to the frying pan and melt. Reduce heat to low and arrange onion wedges in a single layer in the pan, cut-sides down. Cook gently for 10–12 minutes until onions are starting to caramelise on the underside. Add the port/red wine, thyme leaves, sugar and plenty of seasoning. Increase heat to medium-high and bubble for 3–4 minutes, until the alcohol is well reduced, then remove from heat.

4. Arrange the thyme sprigs and sausages in the bottom of the lined tin, then add the tomatoes. Arrange the onion wedges over and in between the sausages, then spoon over the juices from the pan. Lay the pastry circle over the sausages and onions and tuck the edges down into the tin. Brush the top of the pastry lightly with more egg. Cook in oven for 25–30 minutes, or until puffed and golden.

5. Remove from the oven and leave to cool for 5 minutes. Carefully unclip the tin and invert the tart on to a large serving plate or board. Serve in slices.

FREEZE AHEAD
Prepare to end of step 4. Cool
completely in tin, wrap well, then
freeze for up to 1 month. Defrost
in fridge overnight, unwrap and
reheat in an oven preheated to
200°C (180°C fan) mark 6 for
20 minutes, until piping hot.
Complete the recipe
to serve.

Creamy Black Dhal

Swapping the classic urad dal (dhal) for cooked beluga
lentils drastically reduces the cooking time of this dish,
without compromising on its texture and mellow flavour.

50g butter
3 garlic cloves, crushed
½ tsp mild chilli powder
1 tsp garam masala
5cm piece fresh root ginger, peeled and finely grated
2 tbsp tomato purée
2 x 250g pouches beluga lentils
75ml double cream, plus extra to drizzle

TO SERVE
Small handful coriander, roughly chopped
Flatbreads (optional)

Hands-on time: 30 minutes
Cooking time: about 1 hour 10 minutes
Serves 4

PER SERVING (without flatbreads) 375cals,
14g protein, 23g fat (13g saturates), 24g carbs
(2g total sugars), 9g fibre

1. Melt the butter in a large pan (that has a lid)
   over low-medium heat. Stir in the garlic, spices
   and ginger, and cook for 2 minutes, until fragrant.
   Stir in the tomato purée and cook for 2 minutes.

2. Add the lentils and 400ml water. Bring to the
   boil, then reduce heat to low. Cover and cook for
   1 hour, stirring occasionally, until the lentils have
   broken down slightly and the mixture thickens.

3. Stir through the cream and half a teaspoon salt
   and cook, uncovered, over low heat for a few more
   minutes, until warmed through.

4. Divide the dhal among 4 bowls and drizzle
   with a little extra cream. Serve topped with the
   chopped coriander and some flatbreads on
   the side, if you like.

FREEZE AHEAD
Prepare to end of step 3.
Remove from heat and leave to cool
completely before transferring to
a freezer-safe container and freezing
for up to 1 month. Defrost in the
fridge overnight. Gently reheat in
a pan, adding a splash of water if
needed to loosen, until piping hot.
Complete the recipe
to serve.

Baked Chicken Pesto

The lemony and herby breadcrumb topping adds a fresh zing to this indulgent dish. It's ideal for entertaining as you can make it all ahead of time.

6 skinless chicken breasts
125g ball mozzarella (drained weight)
5 tbsp fresh basil pesto
12 sun-dried tomatoes in olive oil, drained
200g crème fraîche
100g full-fat cream cheese
100g dried breadcrumbs
25g Gruyère, finely grated
Finely grated zest 1 lemon
Small handful parsley, finely chopped
1 tbsp olive oil

Hands-on time: 15 minutes
Cooking time: 40 minutes
Serves 6

PER SERVING 469cals, 27g protein, 33g fat (16g saturates), 17g carbs (4g total sugars), 0.3g fibre

FREEZE AHEAD
Once cooked, cool completely, then wrap the dish well and freeze for up to 1 month. To serve, defrost overnight in the fridge and remove the clingfilm. Re-cover with foil and cook in an oven preheated to 200°C (180°C fan) mark 6 for 30 minutes, removing the foil for the final 10 minutes, until piping hot.

1. Preheat oven to 200°C (180°C fan) mark 6. Put a chicken breast on a chopping board and holding your knife parallel to the board, make a horizontal cut into the side of the breast to make a large pocket, being careful not to cut all the way through. Repeat with the other chicken breasts.

2. Cut the mozzarella into 6 slices. Spoon 1 teaspoon pesto into each chicken breast 'pocket', then stuff each with 2 sun-dried tomatoes and a slice of mozzarella. Arrange the chicken in a single layer in an ovenproof serving dish.

3. In a bowl, mix the crème fraîche, cream cheese and remaining pesto together with some seasoning. Spoon the crème fraîche mixture over the chicken. Cover the dish with foil and cook in the oven for 20 minutes.

4. Meanwhile, in a separate bowl, mix the breadcrumbs, Gruyère, lemon zest, parsley and oil with some seasoning.

5. Remove the dish from the oven, remove the foil and sprinkle the breadcrumb mixture over the chicken. Return to the oven, uncovered, for 20 minutes, until cooked through and bubbling. Serve with steamed greens, if you like.

Mixed Bean Stew with Salsa Verde

If you can't find mixed beans, use any other tinned beans, or a combination, that you like.

FOR THE STEW

1 tbsp olive oil
1 red onion, finely sliced
1 fennel bulb, finely sliced
250g cherry tomatoes, halved
2 garlic cloves, crushed
1 tbsp tomato purée
1 tsp mild chilli powder
2 tsp sweet smoked paprika
2 x 400g tins mixed beans, drained and rinsed
750ml vegan vegetable stock
200g Savoy cabbage, roughly chopped

FOR THE SALSA VERDE

25g coriander
25g mint, leaves picked and stalks discarded
1 tbsp capers, drained
1 garlic clove, crushed
1 tsp Dijon mustard
Juice ½ lemon
1 tbsp vegan red wine vinegar
5 tbsp olive oil

Hands-on time: 20 minutes
Cooking time: about 45 minutes
Serves 4

PER SERVING 360cals, 12g protein, 19g fat
(2g saturates), 28g carbs (10g total sugars), 14g fibre

1. For the stew, heat the oil in a large pan over medium heat and cook the onion and fennel for 10 minutes, until softened. Add the tomatoes and fry for 5 minutes, until starting to break down. Add the garlic, tomato purée and spices and fry for a few minutes. Stir in the beans, stock and plenty of seasoning.

2. Bring to the boil, then reduce the heat and bubble gently for 20–25 minutes, stirring occasionally, to reduce slightly. Add the cabbage and cook for 5 minutes more, until tender.

3. Meanwhile, make the salsa verde. Put all the ingredients plus 2 tablespoons water in a food processor and pulse to a chunky consistency. Or finely chop the herbs and capers by hand, mix in a bowl with the garlic, mustard, lemon juice and vinegar, then gradually whisk in the oil, followed by 2 tablespoons water. Season and set aside.

4. Serve the stew with a dollop of salsa verde over each portion.

FREEZE AHEAD
Prepare the stew but do not add the cabbage. Cool, then freeze for up to 1 month. To serve, defrost overnight in the fridge and reheat until piping hot; then add the cabbage and cook for 5 minutes.

Freeze the salsa verde
separately for up to
1 month. Defrost overnight
in the fridge and bring to
room temperature for
1 hour before serving.

Lime and Coriander Fishcakes

These salmon and prawn fishcakes are zesty and fragrant in equal measure. You could swap the salmon for another meaty fish, such as cod.

500g floury potatoes, peeled and cut into 4cm chunks
250g salmon fillets
200g cooked and peeled king prawns, roughly chopped
2 spring onions, finely sliced
Small handful coriander, roughly chopped
2 tbsp sweet chilli sauce
Finely grated zest 2 limes and juice of 1, plus wedges
    to serve
75g dried breadcrumbs
40g desiccated coconut
25g plain flour
2 medium eggs, beaten
Vegetable oil, to fry

Hands-on time: 30 minutes, plus chilling
Cooking time: about 35 minutes
Serves 4

PER SERVING 562cals, 31g protein, 27g fat
(8g saturates), 47g carbs (7g total sugars), 5g fibre

1. Put the potatoes into a large pan, cover with cold water and bring to the boil. Bubble for 10–13 minutes, until tender. Drain thoroughly and leave to steam dry in a colander for 5 minutes. Return the potatoes to the pan and mash with plenty of seasoning until smooth. Set aside to cool slightly.

2. Meanwhile, put the salmon in a medium pan with 400ml water. Bring to the boil over medium heat, then reduce to a gentle simmer and cook for 4–5 minutes, until the fish is opaque and just cooked. Carefully remove with a slotted spoon to a plate lined with kitchen paper. When cool enough to handle, flake into large chunks, discarding the skin (if present).

3. Add the flaked salmon, prawns, spring onions, coriander, sweet chilli sauce, lime zest, juice and plenty of seasoning to the mashed potato. Stir very gently until just combined, avoiding breaking up the salmon too much. Shape into 8 even patties.

4. Mix the breadcrumbs and coconut in a shallow bowl, then put the flour and eggs into 2 separate shallow bowls. Coat each fishcake in flour (tap off the excess), then egg and finally the breadcrumb mixture. Put on a baking tray lined with baking parchment and chill for at least 30 minutes.

5. Heat a thin layer of oil in a large frying pan over medium-high heat and fry the fishcakes for 3–4 minutes per side (in batches if necessary), or until nicely golden. Drain on a plate lined with kitchen paper and keep warm while you fry the second batch.

6. Serve with lime wedges, a green salad and tartare sauce, if you like.

FREEZE AHEAD
Prepare the fishcakes to the end
of step 4. Layer in a freezer-safe
container between baking
parchment and freeze for up
to 1 month. To serve, defrost
overnight in the fridge and
complete the recipe.

Frozen Banoffee Cheesecake

We've swapped flour for ground almonds to make this pud
gluten free. If it doesn't need to be gluten free, you could swap
the brownie base for crushed chocolate biscuits, if you like.

FOR THE BROWNIE BASE
150g unsalted butter, plus extra to grease
100g dark chocolate, roughly chopped
250g caster sugar
50g ground almonds
25g cocoa powder
½ tsp gluten-free baking powder
3 medium eggs, beaten

FOR THE CHEESECAKE
5 large ripe bananas (about 800g – unpeeled weight)
350g cream cheese
200g tinned caramel
150ml double cream
Dark chocolate curls (see GH TIP), to serve (optional)

**Hands-on time: 15 minutes, plus cooling, freezing
  and softening**
Cooking time: about 25 minutes
Serves 10

PER SERVING 597cals, 8g protein, 37g fat (21g
saturates), 57g carbs (55g total sugars), 2g fibre

1. Preheat oven to 190°C (170°C fan) mark 5 and
   grease and line a 20.5cm springform tin with
   baking parchment. For the brownie base, melt
   the butter and chocolate in a medium bowl set
   over a pan of barely simmering water. Remove
   the bowl from the heat and set aside to cool for
   a few minutes. Stir in the remaining brownie
   ingredients, then scrape the mixture into the
   tin and bake for 20–22 minutes until just firm.
   Set aside to cool.

2. Once the brownie has cooled completely, make
   the cheesecake. Peel the bananas and put in a
   food processor with the cream cheese, caramel,
   cream and a pinch of salt. Pulse until smooth
   and combined. Pour over the brownie base and
   smooth to level. Freeze for 4 hours, or until solid.

3. To serve, soften at room temperature for
   15 minutes before removing from the tin and
   decorating with chocolate curls, if using.

GH TIP
To make dark chocolate
curls, spread melted dark
chocolate on to a chilled baking
sheet and chill again until set
firm. Carefully pull a large sharp
knife or palette knife across
the chilled chocolate to
make curls.

FREEZE AHEAD
Once frozen, wrap well and
freeze for up to 1 month.
Complete the recipe
to serve.

Avocado and White Chocolate Ice Cream Cheesecake

Avocado may seem like a strange addition, but it makes for a deliciously rich and creamy dessert.

200g white chocolate, roughly chopped
2 ripe avocados
200g condensed milk
300ml whole milk
Juice 1 lime
2 tbsp vanilla bean paste

Hands-on time: 15 minutes, plus cooling and freezing
Cooking time: about 5 minutes
Makes about 750ml

PER SCOOP 211cals, 4g protein, 12g fat (6g saturates), 21g carbs (21g total sugars), 1g fibre

1. Melt 125g of the white chocolate in a small bowl set over a pan of gently simmering water, stirring occasionally. Remove and set aside to cool slightly.

2. Whizz the avocado flesh, melted white chocolate, condensed milk, milk, lime juice and vanilla in a blender until smooth. Pour into an ice cream machine and churn until frozen. Fold through the remaining 75g chopped chocolate.

3. Scrape into a freezer-proof container, cover and freeze until solid. Soften at room temperature for 5 minutes before serving.

FREEZE AHEAD
Store in the freezer for up to 1 month.

Coconut Chocolate Cheesecake Bombes

These creamy puds are so rich and full of flavour, you'll never guess they don't contain any dairy.

DF

300ml full-fat coconut milk, from a tin
100g caster sugar
150ml coconut whipping cream alternative
1 tbsp vanilla bean paste
2 tbsp coconut rum
75g desiccated coconut
300g dark chocolate, chopped
2 tbsp coconut oil

Hands-on time: 20 minutes, plus freezing and cooling
Cooking time: about 5 minutes
Makes 4

PER BOMBE 782cals, 5g protein, 54g fat (42g saturates), 62g carbs (60g total sugars), 6g fibre

1. Line 4 x 150–175ml dariole moulds or miniature pudding basins with clingfilm, leaving a little excess hanging over the sides.

2. In a large bowl using a handheld electric whisk, beat the coconut milk, sugar, cream alternative and vanilla until slightly thickened and foamy, about 5 minutes. Stir in the rum and 50g of the desiccated coconut and divide between the prepared moulds. Fold over the excess clingfilm to cover and freeze for at least 4 hours, or until set firm.

3. Once set, melt the chocolate and oil in a heatproof bowl set over a pan of barely simmering water, stirring to combine. Remove the bowl from the heat, scrape the chocolate into a wide jug and set aside to cool slightly.

4. Remove the bombes from the moulds, discarding the clingfilm, and arrange on a wire rack set over a baking tray. Dip the base of each bombe into the cooled chocolate and return to the wire rack. Pour the remaining chocolate over the bombes, using a palette knife to help smooth down the sides, if needed, and working quickly as it sets fast. Sprinkle over the remaining dessicated coconut. Serve straight away or return to the freezer.

FREEZE AHEAD
Once the chocolate has set hard, wrap each bomb individually and store in an airtight container. Freeze for up to 1 month.

13

Sweet Things

Plum, Vanilla and White Chocolate Crumble

This super-simple crumble is perfect on a chilly day, with extra white chocolate adding a note of sweetness to the crumble topping.

FOR THE FILLING
750g plums, halved and stoned
50g light brown soft sugar
2 tsp vanilla bean paste

FOR THE TOPPING
175g plain flour
125g butter, chilled and cut into cubes
50g rolled oats
75g demerara sugar
50g white chocolate, roughly chopped

Hands-on time: 10 minutes
Cooking time: about 35 minutes
Serves 6

PER SERVING 474cals, 6g protein, 21g fat
(13g saturates), 64g carbs (36g total sugars), 5g fibre

1. Preheat oven 200°C (180°C fan) mark 6. For the filling, roughly chop the plums and put into a large pan with the sugar, vanilla and 2 tablespoons water. Cover and cook over medium heat for 5 minutes, or until plums are softening. Empty into an ovenproof serving dish.

2. For the topping, put the flour into a bowl and rub in the butter using your fingertips, until the mixture resembles breadcrumbs. Alternatively, pulse the flour and butter in the small bowl of a food processor. Mix in the oats, demerara sugar and white chocolate, then sprinkle the crumble over the fruit layer.

3. Bake for 25-30 minutes, or until the crumble is golden. Serve with custard or ice cream.

3-minute Microwave Chocolate Pudding

This really is the perfect molten chocolate pudding, and it's almost instant!

2½ tbsp cocoa powder
2 tbsp golden syrup
6 tbsp self-raising flour
2½ tbsp caster sugar
1 medium egg
1½ tbsp mild oil
1½ tbsp milk
40g white chocolate, finely chopped

Hands-on time: 2 minutes
Cooking time: 1 minute
Serves 2

PER SERVING 548cals, 11g protein, 20g fat
(6g saturates), 84g carbs (47g total sugars), 3g fibre

1. Divide 1 tablespoon cocoa equally between 2 standard mugs. Add 1 tablespoon golden syrup to each mug, then mix to a paste. Measure the flour, caster sugar and remaining 1½ tablespoons cocoa into a medium bowl. Crack in the egg and add the oil and milk. Mix well, then stir in the white chocolate.

2. Divide the mixture equally between the mugs, then microwave on full power (800W) for 1 minute 10 seconds. Serve in mugs, or turn on to a plate, adding cream or ice cream, if you like.

Fudge and Ginger Puddings

These light, sticky and very moreish puds are perfect for when a sweet craving hits.

(V)

100g unsalted butter, softened, plus extra to grease
100g soft brown sugar
2 medium eggs, beaten
100g self-raising flour
1 tsp baking powder
1 tsp ground ginger
1 tbsp ginger syrup (from a jar of stem ginger)
75g good-quality fudge, chopped
Zest of 1 orange
Stem ginger ice cream, to serve
4 balls stem ginger, chopped
1–2 tbsp toasted flaked almonds, to decorate
Icing sugar, to dust

Hands-on time: 15 minutes
Cooking time: about 20 minutes
Serves 6

PER SERVING (without the ice cream) 366cals,
5g protein, 19g fat (10g saturates), 45g carbs
(30g total sugars), 1g fibre

1. Preheat oven to 190°C (170°C fan) mark 5. Put a baking sheet in the oven to preheat. Grease and line the base of 6 x 8cm ramekins with greaseproof paper. Put the butter and sugar in a bowl and beat with an electric hand whisk until soft and fluffy.

2. Whisk in the beaten eggs, a little at a time. With a metal spoon, fold in the flour, baking powder, ground ginger and ginger syrup, fudge and zest. Spoon into the ramekins, then stand them on a baking sheet. Bake for 15–20 minutes until firm to the touch and a skewer comes out clean.

3. To serve, run a palette knife round the edge of the sponges and turn out on to plates. Remove the greaseproof paper. Spoon a ball of ice cream on top of each sponge and serve decorated with stem ginger, flaked almonds and a generous dusting of icing sugar.

Chocolate Caramel Tart

A gooey filling made from melted Mars bars is the secret to this indulgent tart. Although the Mars bars do take a while to melt, with just three ingredients, this tart is a simple recipe to remember.

FOR THE BASE
275g Mars bars, roughly chopped
125ml double cream
150g cornflakes, roughly crushed

FOR THE FILLING
250g Mars bars, roughly chopped
150ml double cream

Hands-on time: 15 minutes, plus chilling
Cooking time: about 25 minutes
Serves 12

PER SERVING 341cals, 3g protein, 19g fat
(11g saturates), 39g carbs (27g total sugars), 1g fibre

1. Line the base and sides of a 20.5cm round springform tin with baking parchment.

2. For the base, melt the Mars bars and cream in a large heatproof bowl set over a pan of gently simmering water (make sure the base of the bowl does not touch the water). Stir the mixture occasionally, until smooth (this takes a while).

3. Remove the bowl from the heat and stir in the cornflakes, until coated. Spoon most of the cornflake mixture into the prepared tin and press to level with the back of a spoon. Press the remaining mixture neatly up the sides of the tin about 4cm. Chill for 30 minutes to set.

4. Meanwhile, for the filling, in a clean bowl melt the Mars bars, cream and a pinch of fine salt as before (this takes a while). Pour into the cornflake case (still in tin) and chill for about 2 hours to set.

5. Transfer the tart to a cake stand or plate and serve in slices.

GET AHEAD
Make up to 2 days ahead
and chill in its tin.

Pineapple Upside-down Cake

Just three ingredients with no eggs, no butter, no faff!
This juicy cake also ages well and tastes even better the
day after it's made.

FOR THE CARAMEL
100g caster sugar

FOR THE CAKE
435g tin pineapple chunks in juice
200g self-raising flour
100g caster sugar

Hands-on time: 15 minutes, plus cooling
Cooking time: about 35 minutes
Makes 12 squares

PER SQUARE 138cals, 2g protein, 0g fat (0g saturates),
32g carbs (19g total sugars), 1g fibre

TO STORE
Once cool, cover and store
at room temperature for
up to 3 days.

1. Preheat oven to 180°C (160°C fan) mark 4 and
   line a 20.5cm square tin (measured at the base)
   with baking parchment. For the caramel, in a
   small pan heat the sugar and 50ml water over
   low heat, stirring until the sugar dissolves.
   Increase the heat and bubble until a rich caramel
   forms, swirling the pan rather than stirring.

2. Meanwhile, for the cake, drain the tinned
   pineapple, reserving the juice. Arrange the
   pineapple chunks neatly in the base of the lined
   tin (they won't cover the base). Carefully drizzle
   the caramel over the pineapple chunks.

3. In a medium bowl, whisk the flour and sugar
   until combined. Add 150ml of the reserved
   pineapple juice (top up with water if there's
   not enough) and 3 tablespoons water. Whisk
   to combine. Scrape into the tin on top of the
   pineapple and carefully smooth to level.

4. Bake for 25 minutes, or until lightly golden.
   Leave to cool completely in the tin. To serve,
   invert on to a serving plate, peel off the baking
   parchment and cut into 12 rough squares.

Chocolate
Orange Brownies

Fudgy and gooey, these brownies are almost better a few days after they're baked. If you're not a fan of orange chocolate, leave out the zest and use plain milk chocolate instead.

Ⓥ

150g unsalted butter, plus extra, softened, to grease
100g dark chocolate (70% cocoa solids), roughly chopped
3 medium eggs
250g caster sugar
Finely grated zest 1 orange
25g plain flour
45g cocoa powder
100g orange milk chocolate, roughly chopped

Hands-on time: 20 minutes, plus cooling
Cooking time: about 30 minutes
Makes 16 squares

PER SQUARE 228cals, 3g protein, 13g fat
(8g saturates), 25g carbs (23g total sugars), 1g fibre

1. Preheat oven to 180°C (160°C fan) mark 4 and grease and line a 20.5cm square tin with baking parchment.

2. Melt the butter and dark chocolate in a heatproof bowl set over a pan of barely simmering water. Remove the bowl from the heat and leave to cool for 5 minutes.

3. In a large bowl using a handheld electric whisk, beat the eggs and sugar until pale, thick and fluffy. Beat in the cooled chocolate mixture and orange zest. Sift in the flour, cocoa powder and a pinch of fine salt, and fold in using a large metal spoon.

4. Fold in half the orange chocolate. Scrape into the prepared tin, smooth to level, then sprinkle over the remaining orange chocolate.

5. Bake for 25 minutes, or until a crust has formed on top. Leave to cool completely in the tin before transferring to a board and slicing into 16 squares.

GH TIP
You can dig into the brownies as soon as they're cool, but for a neater slice, store for a day before slicing and serving. Cool the brownie completely, then wrap the tin in foil or clingfilm (or use the parchment to transfer the baked brownie to an airtight container).

TO STORE
Keep in an airtight
container at room
temperature for up
to 6 days.

Rhubarb Fool

This simple summer dessert recipe is ready in 30 minutes. Serve the fool with home-made Stem Ginger Biscuits (see below), which are also ready in under 30 minutes.

400g rhubarb, trimmed and cut into 2.5cm chunks
125g golden caster sugar
50ml Grand Marnier or Cointreau (optional)
300ml double cream
500g non-fat Greek yogurt
½ tsp vanilla extract

Hands-on time: 20 minutes
Cooking time: about 10 minutes
Serves 6

PER SERVING 381cals, 10g protein, 27g fat (17g saturates), 27g carbs (25g total sugars), 1g fibre

1. Put the rhubarb in a pan with 75g of the sugar, the liqueur, if using, and 75ml cold water. Bring to the boil, then simmer gently for 5 minutes. Strain the rhubarb, reserving the syrup.

2. Pour the syrup back into the pan and simmer until reduced by a third. Set aside to cool.

3. Whisk the cream, yogurt, vanilla and the rest of the sugar until soft peaks form. Mash half the rhubarb and stir into the cream, then fold in the remaining pieces. Divide among 6 x 250ml glasses and serve with the syrup.

Stem Ginger Biscuits

These double-ginger biscuits can be served with the Rhubarb Fool (see above) or ice cream, but are equally delicious on their own. Best of all, they're ready just in 30 minutes.

40g golden caster sugar
75g unsalted butter
2½ tbsp golden syrup
175g plain flour
½ tsp ground ginger
40g finely chopped stem ginger

Hands-on time: 10 minutes
Cooking time: about 20 minutes
Makes 18 biscuits

PER BISCUIT 86cals, 1g protein, 4g fat (2g saturates), 13g carbs (6g total sugars), 0.4g fibre

1. Heat 25g of the sugar gently in a pan with the butter and syrup. Mix the flour and ground ginger in a bowl. Take the pan off the heat, add the stem ginger, then stir the syrup into the flour.

2. Pinch off walnut-sized pieces of dough and arrange them 2.5cm apart on non-stick baking sheets. Flatten slightly, then gently press a fork into each biscuit. Sprinkle over the remaining 15g sugar and bake for 15–18 minutes until golden. Leave for a few minutes, then transfer to a wire rack to cool. Serve with the Rhubarb Fool (see above), if you like.

Lemon and Almond Cake

This zesty cake couldn't be easier. Toasting the almonds
first helps to bring out their flavour. You can use regular
self-raising flour if your cake doesn't need to be gluten free.

200g ground almonds
300g gluten-free self-raising flour
500g lemon curd, plus 2 tbsp
2 tbsp flaked almonds

Hands-on time: 15 minutes, plus cooling
Cooking time: about 55 minutes
Serves 8

PER SERVING 500cals, 11g protein, 20g fat
(2g saturates), 67g carbs (34g total sugars), 2g fibre

1. Preheat oven to 180°C (160°C fan) mark 4 and
   line a 20.5cm round springform tin with baking
   parchment. Spread the ground almonds on a
   baking tray and cook in the oven for 10 minutes,
   until fragrant and light golden.

2. Tip the ground almonds into a large bowl (no
   need to cool) and whisk in the flour and a pinch
   of fine salt. In a jug, whisk the 500g lemon curd
   with 200ml just-boiled water. Pour into the flour
   mixture. Briefly whisk until just combined (try
   not to overmix).

3. Scrape into the prepared tin and smooth to level.
   Sprinkle over the flaked almonds and bake for
   45 minutes, or until golden and a skewer inserted
   into the centre comes out clean. Dollop on the
   2 tablespoons lemon curd and brush it over
   the top of the cake to glaze.

4. Leave the cake to cool in the tin for 15 minutes,
   then transfer to a cake stand or serving plate.
   Serve just warm or at room temperature in slices.

TO STORE
Once cool, keep in an
airtight container at room
temperature for up
to 2 days.

Peach, Thyme and Ricotta Galette

We used tinned peaches in this rustic-looking tart for speed, but you can use 6 ripe peaches (peeled, stoned and sliced) or chopped peaches, if you prefer. Sprinkling the cornflour mixture over the fruit helps to thicken any juices.

320g sheet puff pastry
250g ricotta
2 tbsp runny honey
2 x 410g tin peach halves, drained
2 tbsp caster sugar, plus extra to sprinkle
1 tbsp cornflour
2 thyme sprigs, leaves picked

Hands-on time: 15 minutes
Cooking time: about 20 minutes
Serves 8

PER SERVING 260cals, 6g protein, 13g fat
(7g saturates), 30g carbs (16g total sugars), 1g fibre

1. Preheat oven to 220°C (200°C fan) mark 7. Unroll the pastry on to a baking sheet (leaving it on the baking parchment).

2. In a food processor, or in a medium bowl using a whisk, whizz/beat the ricotta and honey until smooth. Spread over the pastry, leaving a 3cm border. Slice each peach half into 5 wedges and arrange on top of the ricotta mixture.

3. In a small bowl, mix the sugar, cornflour and thyme. Sprinkle over the filling. Fold in the pastry border and sprinkle a little caster sugar over the border. Bake for 20 minutes, or until the pastry is golden and crisp. Cut into slices and serve.

Hermit Cookie Squares

Full of comforting spice and dried fruit, this is an easy version of a New England staple that is somewhere between a brownie and a chewy American cookie in texture.

150g block margarine/vegetable shortening/plant butter
  alternative, softened, plus extra to grease
200g light brown soft sugar
125g black treacle
2 tsp ground mixed spice
1 medium egg
175g raisins
250g self-raising flour

Hands-on time: 15 minutes, plus cooling
Cooking time: about 20 minutes
Makes 15 squares

PER SQUARE 240cals, 3g protein, 8g fat (3g saturates), 39g carbs (26g total sugars), 1g fibre

1. Preheat oven to 180°C (160°C fan) mark 4 and grease and line a 27 x 39cm lipped baking tray with baking parchment.

2. In a large bowl, using a handheld electric whisk, beat the margarine/shortening/butter alternative, sugar, treacle, mixed spice and ¼ teaspoon fine salt until slightly paler in colour and fluffy, about 3 minutes. Add the egg, beat again briefly, then add the raisins and flour and beat until combined.

3. Scrape on to the prepared tray and spread to level with a spatula. Bake for 15–20 minutes, or until just firm to the touch and a toothpick inserted into the centre comes out clean (it will continue to firm up as it cools). Leave to cool in the tray before cutting into 15 rough squares.

TO STORE
Keep in an airtight container at room temperature for up to 1 week.

Index